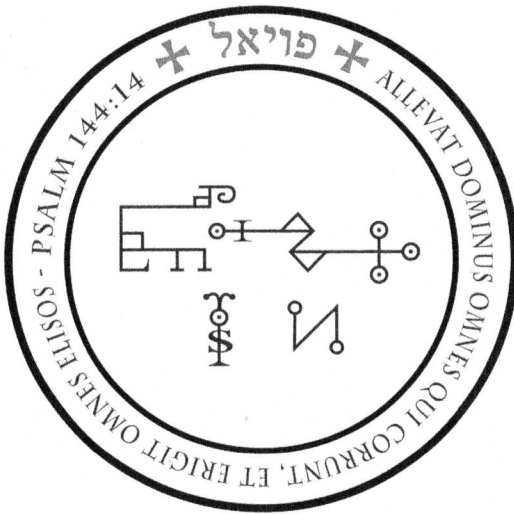

פויאל

PSALM 144:14

ALLEVAT DOMINUS OMNES QUI CORRUUNT, ET ERIGIT OMNES ELISOS

THE INSTITUTE FOR HERMETIC STUDIES

STUDY GUIDE XI

RITUAL PURIFICATION, EXORCISM & DEFENSIVE MAGIC

A Transcription of Lectures Presented by

MARK STAVISH, M.A.

IHS FOUNDER & DIRECTOR OF STUDIES

∞

ALFRED DeSTEFANO III

SERIES EDITOR

Ritual Purification, Exorcism, & Defensive Magic

IHS Study Guide Series
Volume XI

Copyright © 2018 Mark Stavish

Transcription, editing, and typesetting by
~ Alfred DeStefano III ~

The sigil of Poiel at the front of this book was created by
~ Fr. John Kadai ~

Email: info@hermeticinstitute.org
Website: www.hermeticinstitute.org

Also by Mark Stavish:

- *Egregores: The Occult Entities That Watch Over Human Destiny*
- *The Path of Alchemy: Energetic Healing and the World of Natural Magic* (Available in Polish and Russian)
- *Kabbalah for Health and Wellness* (First Edition & Second Revised, Updated Edition; available in Portuguese and Russian)
- *Freemasonry: Rituals, Symbols, and History of the Secret Society* (Available in French, Portuguese, Spanish, and Estonian)
- *Between the Gates: Lucid Dreaming, Astral Projection, and the Body of Light in Western Esotericism* (Available in Portuguese, Russian, and French)
- *The Magical World of Dr. Joseph Lisiewski*
- *Voice of Hermes: Lessons from the Path*
- *Light on the Path: A Study Guide for Qabala, Alchemy & Astrology* (IHS Study Guides, Volume I)
- *The Inner Way: The Power of Prayer and Belief in Spiritual Practice* (IHS Study Guides, Volume II)
- *Child of the Sun: Psychic & Physical Rejuvenation in Alchemy and Qabala* (IHS Study Guides, Volume III)
- *Words of My Teachers: A Companion to the IHS Audio Programs* (IHS Study Guides, Volume IV)
- *Unfolding the Rose: Illumination & Western Esotericism* (IHS Study Guides, Volume V)
- *Mind of Hermes: Visionary Experiences in Western Esotericism* (IHS Study Guides, Volume VI)
- *Pathology of the Sublime: Problems & Solutions on the Spiritual Journey* (IHS Study Guides, Volume VII)
- *Sanctus: The Spirituality of Daily Life* (IHS Study Guides, Volume VIII)
- *The Four Aims: Jupiter in Daily Living* (IHS Study Guides, Volume IX)
- *Pow-Wow: Traditional Folk & Grimoire Magic of the Pennsylvania German Magi* (IHS Study Guides, Volume X)

Continued on the following page...

- *The Liturgy of Hermes: In Praise of the Lord of Light* (IHS Ritual Series, Volume I)
- *Meditations & Rituals* (IHS Ritual Series, Volume II)

The IHS Monograph Series by Mark Stavish:

- *Introduction to Hermeticism: Its Theory & Practice*

- *The Theory & Practice of Enochian Magic*

- *Drawing Down the Life of Heaven: An Introduction to Renaissance Magic*

- *How to Develop Your Psychic Abilities*

- *Mercury's Children: Shamanic & Hermetic Practices*

- *Studies in Poltergeists, Obsession & Possession*

- *Wisdom's Bliss & Khamael's Spear*

- *Introduction to Alchemy: A Golden Dawn Perspective*

- *Rosicrucianism for the New Millenium: 400th Anniversary Edition*

- *Pietism, Pow-Wow & the Magical Revival*

Contents

⟋ ACKNOWLEDGMENTS ⟍

This book and the seminar it is based upon would not be possible if it were not for the support of Brian Osborne of Emerald Flame, who first suggested and sponsored a weekend retreat in the summer of 2013, and Alfred DeStefano III, who has steadfastly dedicated his time and enormous talent to editing, proofreading, typesetting, and even transcribing not only this book in particular, but all IHS work in general. There are of course the many "unknowns" who have supported our work in various ways: our patrons, invisible guardians and associates from the other side who have cleared away obstacles to our work, and our readers in general. Thanks to each of you. There is—and this is most important—the support given to me and this work by my wife Andrea and our sons Luke and Nathaniel. If it were not for their long, patient suffering at times, none of this would be possible.

As such, I dedicate the energy of awakening this publication creates—and from its use by all those known and unknown, visible and invisible who benefit from it—to the health and prosperity of everyone who has had a hand in its creation.

Notice: Please do not read this book in the bathroom or any unclean place. If it is to be disposed of, please do so by burying it directly in the earth, preferably where it has been sanctified, or by burning it to complete ash, along with powerful and potent herbs, so that not even a single letter or symbol remains, as an offering to the wellness of all beings.

✠ ✠ ✠

~ INTRODUCTION ~

The following book is derived from the transcripts of a presentation given on 17-18 August 2013 near Plattsburgh, New York. Attendees traveled from across the United States and Canada to take part. A complete recording of the program was made available for those who could not attend; this was eventually placed on the Internet for students to listen to for free. However, like all recordings of live events, quality of the presentation is fluid, as is the physical recording itself. Some points are clearer than others and topics were inevitably discussed when the recording was not being made. To smooth out and better codify the presentation of the materials, the present study guide is being published.

This book is part of a series designed to give the reader a strong foundation in theoretical and practical esotericism. Readers will benefit from the contents herein by studying it with the material presented in *Words of My Teachers: A Companion to the IHS Audio Programs* (IHS Study Guides, Vol. IV) and *Unfolding the Rose: Illumination & Western Esotericism* (IHS Study Guides, Vol. V). Several volumes from the IHS Monograph Series will also be helpful: *Drawing Down the Life of Heaven: An Introduction to Renaissance Magic, Mercury's Children: Shamanic & Hermetic Practices*, and *Studies in Poltergeists, Obsession & Possession*.

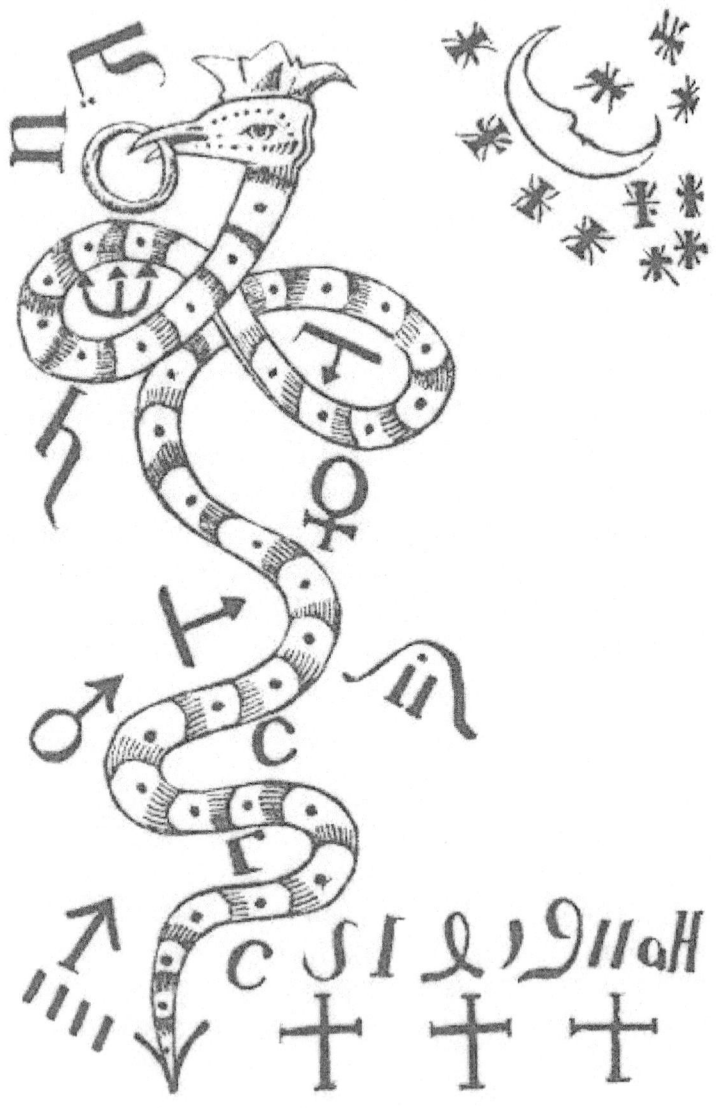

◇ PART ONE ◇

You can see that to the left of me is a small altar. We have our three candles: the Trinity of Lights, the Holy Trinity, the Holy Upper Trinity. We have a small candle to the right of me, before an empty chair, which represents the Invisible Light made manifest and the manifest made invisible; that is the chain of initiation and tradition. It is what we call the "Unknown" or "Invisible Master." It's not just a person—it is a whole archetype. And it's not just an archetype that is an abstraction of our imagination, but it's a very real thing.

Relax and, within your own mind, recite with me as I say our prayer. This is a prayer to what we call the "Chain of Light" and the "Chain of Initiation," our connection to a tradition—not just *now*, not just something of the present. Something that goes *back*, and if all goes well, goes *forward* as well.

> Eternal, Ineffable God, Holy Father of all things, Thou who sees and embraces everything. Answer the prayer of Thy servants prostrate before Thee. Give us the contemplation, the fervor, and the sincerity necessary for the sentiments that we wish to express today. Be auspicious for us, O Ineffable Father, for me and for all those men and women for whom I have come to intercede, and for my Brethren on the Path of Return. For my parents, for my friends, for my enemies, for the living and the dead, and for all of Thy creatures, O Merciful Lord. So answer me, O my God; grant to me the gift to pray to Thee efficiently. Here I now surrender to Thy Holy Guard. So have pity on me and may Thy Will be done. Amen.

And now O my Patrons of Spirits, freed of material ties; Thou who henceforth enjoy the fruits of Thy virtues and whose Names I am lucky to carry, I beseech Thee! By the Name that Thou Thyselves have invoked with so much fervor, confidence, and success, I beseech Thee to contribute to my eternal salvation by Thy Holy Intercession and by Thy Protection, with the Father of Mercy and Reconcilers and Conservatory Spirit. Obtain for me and for all of my Brethren the Mercy of the Divinity, whose favor is His Clemency and that rewards Thee now for all of those fights which Thou have given in this place where I still am. Ensure by Thy beneficial assistance that I live and I shall die as Thee, in Peace, in Joy, in Holiness. Amen.

And Thou, O Pure Spirit, my Guardian, put in charge by the Eternal One to watch over me, and for the entire reconciliation of my spiritual being, I implore Thee, in the Name of the God of Mercy, come to the assistance of my soul! Every time that it may be in danger of succumbing to evil; every time and it will call Thee by its desires, its sighs, and its meditations; every time that it will be hungry and thirsty for advice, for instruction, and for understanding. So help me, O my Guardian! Obtain the protection and assistance of the Patrons, Whom I have just invoked, as also the submissiveness of the spirits whom I should have called up in this operation. Help me therefore; help in my poverty and in my nakedness, and in all of my needs. Amen.

Our Father Who art in Heaven, hallowed be Thy Name. Thy Kingdom come, Thy Will be done, on Earth as it is in Heaven. Give us this day our daily bread, and forgive us our trespasses as we forgive those who trespass against us. Deliver us from temptation and deliver us from evil. For Thine is the Kingdom and the Power and the Glory, forever and ever. Amen.

He that dwells in the secret place of the Most High shall abide under the shadow of the Almighty. I will say of the Lord, He is my refuge and my fortress, my God in Whom I trust. Surely he shall deliver thee from the snare of the fowler and from the noisome pestilence. He shall cover thee with His feathers and under His wings thou shalt trust; His truth shall be thy shield and buckler. Thou shalt not be afraid for the terror of the night, nor the arrow that flieth by day, nor the pestilence that walks in darkness, nor the destruction that wasteth at noon-day. A thousand shall fall at thy side, and ten thousand at thy right hand, but it shall not come nigh thee, for only with thine eyes shalt thou behold and see the rewards of the wicked. Because thou hast made the Lord which is my refuge, even the Most High, thy habitation, no evil shall befall thee, neither shall any plague come nigh thy dwelling. For He shall give His Angels charge over thee, to keep thee in all thy ways. They shall bear thee up in their hands lest thou dash thy foot against a stone. Thou shalt tread upon the lion and the adder; the young lion and the dragon shalt thou trample under foot. Because he hath set his love upon Me, therefore I will deliver him. I will set him on high because he hath known My Name. He shall call upon Me and I will answer him; I will be with him in trouble and I will deliver him and honor him. With long life will I satisfy him and show him My salvation.

Glory be to the Father and to the Son and to the Holy Spirit. As it was in the beginning, is now, and ever shall be, world without end. Amen.

We have talked a great deal about our relationship to others and that if we want to transform ourselves into the glorious "Body of Light" that is spoken about in the scriptures and in Agrippa—we'll go over some of those quotes in his *Third Book*—we have to develop a certain quality within ourselves, and that quality is *genuine compassion*. It is a sincere and genuine relationship to others.

And these others are not limited to those in our immediate circle. That's a nice place to start, but it doesn't end there. It is to *all living beings*.

That prayer which I just read to you—what does it say? "For my parents, my friends, my enemies, the living, the dead; for all Thy creatures, O Merciful Lord." This is a wonderful Catholic prayer. It comes under the French occult tradition, which tends to be Roman Catholic in orientation. But we see the *same* notions stated in the Orthodox tradition, particularly the Desert Fathers, which is really nice because this was going on at the same time the Hermetic Tradition was going on.

As some of you may know, up until the mid-Renaissance, Hermes was considered a co-equal of Moses. So Hermes wasn't really cast out of the social/spiritual spectrum until fairly late in the game. In fact, some of the ceilings in the Vatican have his picture on them.

That said, let's look at one of the prayers from St. Isaac the Syrian:

> What is a merciful heart? It is a heart burning for the sake of the entire Creation; for men, for birds, for animals, for demons, and for every created thing. And by the recollection and sight of them, the eyes of a merciful man pour forth abundant tears from the strong and vehement mercy which grips his heart. And from this great compassion, his heart is humbled, and he cannot bear to see or hear any injury or slight sorrow in Creation.
>
> For this reason he continually offers up tearful prayers even for the irrational beasts, for the enemies of Truth, and for those who harm him, that they may be protected and receive mercy. And in like manner, he even prays for the family of reptiles because of the great compassion that burns in his heart without

measure in the likeness of God.[1]

I bring this up because there are many ways to look at scriptures. There's what we call an *Outer* or *Exoteric* understanding, where the scripture is interpreted literally. "It's a historical fact."

Then there's a quasi-esoteric interpretation where we look at it in terms of allegory and moral teaching. The churches have done a fairly decent job of that in some ways. But you notice that it moves away from a historical, outer meaning to one that is personal: "How does this relate to *me*?"

Then we move into not just that moral and allegorical teaching but to another level, as we stated last time, and that is where these teachings take on a very symbolic level and have to do with our progress on what we call the Path of Return: spiritual integration (we call it "unfoldment"). Illumination.

And there's a final level which is how the scriptures relate, simply, to "Absolute Truth." It is really a *direct revelation* within the mind of "absoluteness."

None of these are in contradiction to one another, even if they appear to be so, because their fundamental aim is all the same: the improvement of the human condition. Each of us looks at them differently, because—as we said—we may all be *created* equal, but we're *not* all equal! We all have different *expressions*, and skills, and qualities, and understandings; we're at different stages of our growth. So the teachings that are of immense value to someone on one level, may have *no* meaning to someone on another, and may actually be a *lie*.

To tell someone the truth before they're ready for it is the same as lying to them. They can't process it. And that's what proselytizers don't understand.

So, you have to recognize that the work *you're* doing is very much an *inner, personal* work. It's about *your* re-integration—and we'll talk about that a little more.

---

[1] St. Isaac the Syrian, Homily 81.

The problem with that is, though, it has this wonderful habit of becoming *terribly* narcissistic! What I mean by that is—and you've all done it—*we've* all done it! It's *wonderful!* We get *so* caught up in our *own* spiritual pursuits—because *we're* just *too good* for getting our hands dirty! [laughter]— that we lose touch with others.

And that's okay! Because in the beginning, so much of our world is externally motivated, because—as I've said to many of you—we really don't appreciate the kind of god-realm that we live in. Everything is so *fast* and *easy.* We think it was always that way, when it was not.

Up until recently, life was very hard. Very short and often very brutal. We're very fortunate that we have the *time* and the *wealth* and the *resources* to come together like this as a group to learn. Really, very fortunate! You have to appreciate that. And often that isn't appreciated because we take it for granted that we can have "whatever we want whenever we want it."

It's kind of funny, when I talk to my eighteen-year-old. I've said: "You're the first generation that's *willfully* walked around with its head down!" I'm talking both literally and metaphorically; they don't get it—*well,* one of them gets it.

My children are so funny. They want me to order stuff online. So I say, "What do you want? It will be here in three days. When I was your age and I ordered stuff, the coupon we had to fill out and send in said: 'Allow four to six weeks for delivery'!" [laughter]

[Audience Member:] And we were okay with that!

We were okay with that! [laughter] That was the joy of waiting. So we have to look at our life and the environment we're in and ask: "How is this environment affecting our perceptions of ourselves and others?" It makes us very *selfish.* We're spiritually selfish. And when you *understand* that you're spiritually selfish—just as when you understand when you are materially selfish, emotionally selfish, fill-in-the-blank—when you *realize* that, you say: "I get it. I don't feel good about that, but now I can change it.'"

It's not about beating yourself up—it's about realization. Change it. How do I make things better for myself? Well, one of the ways is by making them better for *others*. You are not—and this is a tricky metaphysical distinction—we like to say "we're all 'One,' " but we're not. What we are is *interdependent* on one another; we all *interact* with one another. That is: anything that I do has a potential to impact on anyone. Anything *you* do has a potential to impact on *me*. So my thoughts and prayers have a potential to affect you, just as your thoughts and prayers have a potential to affect me, and all these other things.

I say that because it's *in potential*. There has to be a *receptivity* to it. If we were all "One," then there would be no potential—it would just be a done deal.

I say this so that we're very clear, since often we use language in metaphysics that is not necessarily accurate. It's nice to speak of "the Oneness, the Oneness, the Oneness"— but that's not completely accurate. It's more subtle than that, particularly as far as we're concerned. Because in magical acts, occult acts, we deal with those potentials. As my great-uncle used to say: "Man proposes, but God disposes." [laughter]

That's why in German folk magic they say "I'll try." Because we don't know what will happen, a lot of times. Isn't that the great joke? "Yeah, magic always works—we're just not sure *how*!" [laughter] Okay! I'll give that a shot—let's see what happens... Oh! Where's that fire extinguisher?!? [laughter] Did you get that on film?!?

So we really open ourselves up, and we *need* to open ourselves up to others, to one another. And we need to do that on a meaningful level. At the end of the last class I talked to you about the *blue light* and the *blue man* spoken of by Hildegard and mentioned by Paracelsus—perhaps also by Agrippa. That's interesting because the inner deities are often painted or portrayed as blue because it means *openness*—sky, vastness. In the Masonic Lodge, the first three degrees are known as the "Blue Lodge." The sky—vast; but also the canopy of heaven. Blue is the color of Jupiter, of Chesed, and Chesed is the Sphere of *Mercy*—the mercy we just invoked in our prayer.

When we pray or meditate, it's interesting to look back and reflect on how often you include others in your operation or prayer. There's a section from the *Corpus Hermeticum* which I used to do regularly. I would read it out; "imagine this" and "imagine that" and all this stuff—and then I say to you: "So, when you're visualizing all that, how many of you were *alone*?"

Inevitably, every class, everyone!

It's true—we think only of ourselves. Even in the great pursuit of our illumination: "It's for *me!*" There are some schools of thought that say that your job is to find illumination, which is the Inner Light. That's what we'll talk about on an esoteric level. Illumination refers to the Inner Light—the Inner Light of what we call "enlightenment." It is *literally* a "filling with light," by the way. *Literally*—not just figuratively.

From illumination we get—in these terms—*salvation*. We want our salvation. It's an understanding; it's an experience; it's the re-integration; it's *unity*. It's the transcendence of duality. It can happen when you're *dead*; it can happen while you're *alive*. Doesn't matter. It's having overcome that sense of either-or/this-or-that/me-you.

Still I understand that I exist, but the question is *where do you fit into my worldview*? And where do I fit into yours?

So let us close our eyes, and breathe deep, and relax, and reach *out*...or reach *down*...into our heart.

And notice that small, blue sphere of light that is there.

And it is not just there as if you're *looking* at it—you are *there inside of it.*

And allow it to *expand* and *fill out* and *fill you*. Let it fill you. Fill the room. Now, fill everyone else in the room. These are your friends; these are your co-workers on the Path. These are your brothers and sisters. These are the members of the Household of the Faithful.

And now let it reach out and think of your parents. Your brothers. Your sisters. Particularly if you don't have a good relationship with them—you need it all the more. Bring them into it.

And bring in all those people that you saw on your way here. The ones you paid when you got your gas or stopped to eat or walked by. People you see every day. People you have a relationship with but really don't think much about.

Now let it reach out...and continue...just creeping...at a nice, steady pace...filling out, reaching out, across the globe. And take your time with this.

All the people in your past. All the people in your present. All the potential people in your future. They're all there with you. They're all there, in your heart. And there's *room* for them.

Make sure you bring up the people you like...and make sure to bring up the people who've given you much pain. And bring them all there.

And of course the people who are neutral. The girl at the cash register. And the busboy. And this man that walks by.

See them all there. And see *them* filled with this blue light, and happy, too, and expanding *their* hearts, just as you are expanding yours.

Feel the joy. This is *so* important! *Feel the joy.* We talk of this as Light, Life, and Love; the Holy Trinity of Rosicrucianism. It's *Light*, it's *Life*, it's *Love*. Great joy.

That is what real salvation is: salvation is bliss—bliss is joy. Joy is love. That is unity. That is the One.

Reach this out to your animals, the ones you have, the ones you've seen, the ones that are out there. The birds, the fish, the creeping things. Things which walk. Things which fly, and swim. Reach out to the invisible energies and entities; the energies of Earth and Air, Fire and Water. The so-called "Elementals" that are within our bodies, that we must make a healthy relationship with; that are within the earth and the whole physical universe itself.

Through all this—the earth, the physical universe—the Elements are there.

Reach out to the dead. Those joyfully experiencing some heavenly state. And wish that they awaken even further on their Path. Feel them doing so. And reach out to those who suffer—the dead who wander. These, we say, are in "purgatory" or "limbo" of some kind. Ghosts wander. Wish that they will find happiness and joy—this Divine Mercy. This Divine Abundance—this cornucopia.

Whatever they seek—whatever *any* of them seek—they will have.

And imagine yourself giving it to them. Each and every one of them—all of them. They may want wisdom and insight. They may simply want something to eat, just as the bird does, or the reptile. They may just want to feel safe; they may want all sorts of material goods, emotional states—all of these are what they desire to feel happy.

And wish it for them. And see yourself giving it to them.

Books for those who want to learn; water for those who want to drink; clothes for those who wish for clothes. Healing medicine for those who are sick. The list goes on—it is endless. And so is the potential to fill.

Reach out now, up into the heavenly realms—for even there, there are beings of great, spiritual power, who still have not achieved the final liberation, the final insight. Pray for them, and wish for them that *they* will be happy, and that all those on the Path will achieve the Supreme Illumination, that supreme salvation or transcendence that they desire. Wish it for them as well as for yourself and for others.

And reach down into the pits of hell, where there are those who suffer and walk upside-down, as they say in the Egyptian scriptures. Where there is nothing but chaos and torment, and great suffering of unspeakable magnitude. Reach down in there with your heart and this light. And reach out to them—that all of them may find happiness and peace and joy.

And allow this light to pour forth from you to all these dimensions, all these realms, all these places, [nothing is without it]. And rest in it.

> When the Spirit takes its dwelling-place in man, he does not cease to pray, because the Spirit will continually pray in him. And neither when he sleeps, nor when he's awake, will prayer be cut off from his soul. And when he eats and when he drinks, lies down, or when he does anything—even when he is immersed in sleep—the perfumes of prayer will breathe in his heart spontaneously.[2]

Too often, when we think of our work, we think of our work as a *thing that we do*: "I *must* draw this circle... I *must* meditate on *this*... I *must* memorize *that*..." When, really, the work is the work of the *heart*. It is our compassion and strength as a human being.

Those "Invisible Masters" which we hear so much about or are told about—the "Chain of Initiation" comes, we are told, down from Chesed, from Mercy. If we wish to be like *them*— if we wish to be like God—then we must be all-expansive. But: compassionate with *wisdom*, too, as our prayer says: understanding. We are not *foolish* in it.

Even Jesus said: "Go help people! But if they don't want to hear the Gospel, don't waste your time—leave!" There's a difference between being a *teacher* and being a *reformer*. [laughter] A teacher's work is done; a reformer's work is *never* done! [laughter] And in their desire to create Heaven on Earth, they make Hell. There's "always one more thing to fix."

Well, there's nothing to fix anyhow, in many ways. Enlightenment isn't some state that you aspire to—it's a state

---

[2]A. J. Wensinck (trans.), *Mystic Treatises by Isaac of Nineveh: Translated from Bedjan's Syriac Text with an Introduction and Registers* (Amsterdam: Uitgave der Koninklijke Akademie van Wetenschappen, 1923) 174.

that you uncover *right now.* We just keep thinking, "I'll get my illumination *later.*" Later, later: "at some point." It's some "ethereal thing." It's *not.* It's *right here,* within you—you just have to *stop, relax,* and *enter into yourself* in a very, very simple manner.

You notice that's what the great mystics of the past have always done, and it gave rise to these "great visions." It gave rise like with Jacob Boehme or Saint John—all of them had all these great visions. And then people took these great visions and they either said, "We don't like them!" Or they said, "We don't like them, but we can *use* them!"

And then they turn them into doctrines. That's why I say that esotericism is both the *seed* and the *fruit* of religion. One's mystical experience is the seed that gives rise to a religious or outer experience; one's inner experience individually gives rise to an outer, collective religious experience or practice. Which then, in turn—if properly done—gives rise to an *inner* mystical experience within the individual.

But from our esoteric viewpoint, there's no such thing as "collective salvation." There's no such thing as "collective rising above duality," because it's *individual* work. It is the purpose of the Great Work that each person shall perfect their own powers, for themselves. Otherwise, there would be no such thing as free will—no choice.

The question then is, "What do we do?" How do we deal with these contradictions or apparent contradictions? Well, *there aren't any there.* I undertake the Work in and of and for myself; along the way, I do my best to help those who are "helpable."

Although we don't like to say it, the reality is that you can educate ignorance, but you can't educate "stupid!" [laughter] If you can't recognize that someone can't understand what you're teaching, then you *should* be frustrated! [laughter] But if you recognize that someone needs your help or *can* benefit or *might be able to* benefit, then you go help them—but you help them for the sake of helping *them,* not for yourself.

Now, you may say, "You know what? I'm going to just give this a try—let's see what happens!" [laughter] That's one thing; but how do we help? We help *in silence*, meaning that we do it *quietly*.

To truly be helpful requires a strong degree of anonymity. You simply go about your work and do it. You're looking for compassion and generosity to all, without reward or "the glory of it."

I was talking to some folks the other night and even over the week about this very topic. They said, "Well, how can I help?" Because what they see as "helping" is either walking around with a sign somewhere, telling other people what to do—which isn't help; or complaining—which isn't help; or some kind of grandiose, one-shot deal. Often people want to help in *big* ways, with grandiose schemes, "world salvation." "Save the whales!"

That's good and all, but is it within your capacity? Even Jesus Christ couldn't save the world. Even the Buddha said, "Within five hundred years my teachings will become decadent." So you have to be *honest* with what is in your capacity—but that's okay, because we have a thing called *leverage*.

"Leverage" means—well, Albert Einstein said that the eighth wonder of the world was compound interest! [laughter] That's what we're talking about: compound interest. Little things done well add up. You know that. Little things done well add up; they make a big difference.

For an example, I'm on the board of a library—a small one, some of you have been there. What makes a difference in our budget at the end of the year would have *absolutely, positively no impact* in other organizational budgets. None! None whatsoever!

I tell people: "If you'd really like your donation to make a big splash, you have to throw it in a small pond!" [laughter]

We're a small pond! Your five hundred or one thousand dollars—"it's not so much, I can't send so much"—wait a minute! Hold on! You're right. Fifty bucks isn't a lot. But if I get fifty from *ten* of you, that's five hundred; if I get another five hundred from this fund over here, that's a thousand. If I get thirteen hundred, I've got one percent of my organization's annual budget. You've just saved us a lot of time and energy because of what our spending requirements are to stay certified as a library.

So, your fifty dollars means two books we don't have to buy to stay accredited. Your fifty dollars doesn't really mean a whole lot when it's given to "x–y–z." You've got to put it in perspective if bang for your buck is what you're looking for. It's up to you. You decide what you want to do. I'm just telling you how this will affect us.

Same thing in your daily life when you are going out to help people. When is it going to give you bang for your buck? How is it you're going to get leverage? A little bit each day. It all adds up, if you do it carefully.

People don't change quickly—that's okay. So we have to look long term. This is very, very important, because without compassion, the universe has no reason to help you. The universe is looking for bang for its buck. Jean Dubuis was funny about this; he'd say, "You know, the universe puts a lot of energy into keeping you here!" It's true. So, what's it getting for its investment?

I don't teach you simply so you can get "happiness" and "joy." I teach you so you can get happiness and joy and hopefully keep that moving forward. I want some bang for my buck! I want some return on my investment.

If you notice, spiritual traditions were all that way. They're looking for people who would not just be concerned about themselves, but concerned about themselves in a healthy way, so that they can, in turn, help others in a healthy way. We call that: compassion, the mercy of Chesed.

We also talked about the importance of having confidence in the teachings and helping your fellow students, which we call by the Hermetic phrase "the household of the faithful." We're brothers and sisters here; we need to treat each other as such, and help each other along the journey, because the teachings are put in practice first and foremost *right here*. Without that practice, it doesn't matter what I say to you, or what is written in books—that just becomes dead. It's only in your individual life that they stay alive.

We talked about the four powers of the Adept—and I say these for lack of better terms, because we don't have a great codified terminology in Western esotericism, that's important to note. They are *exorcism, enchantment, expansion*, and *eradication*.

Exorcism is like "washing the plate"—getting rid of the "dirty things." Healing, essentially; sweeping the way.

Enchantment is magnetism, to bring those things that are desirable to you or others.

Expansion is pushing outward. We have to continually expand our powers, our presence of being, our state of mind.

Eradication is complete removal of any obstacles—and those obstacles are primarily obstacles of the mind. Your false, limiting, petty notions of yourself.

What does it say in the *Corpus Hermeticum*? "But if one thinks 'I can't do this' and 'I can't do that'..." [laughter] Well, you're never going to be equal to God. [laughter] How often haven't you *whined* out your prayers to God? "Oh, *please* God! Oh, *please* help me! I'm a good boy or girl! Why does this crap happen to me?!?" [laughter]

You know!

It is a double-edged sword, truly. One of the things that Brian Osborne (our host) and I talked about at length is the notion of *systems*, and how you have systems that are concerned with *principles* or *formulas*. He gave a great quote from one of his teachers, a Taoist instructor, who said: "Formulas or techniques are like keys that can unlock a particular lock." This is wonderful, because if you have a lot of formulas, you can open a lot of locks. But then the question is how many keys can you carry with you?

We've all seen that maintenance guy or security person...

[laughter] Or *ourselves!* "How many keys do I *have* here?" That's why people end up saying: "I just use one password for *everything!*" [laughter]

I don't *care* if they get in! I just can't find them if I don't write them down! [laughter] Or I write down my passwords and then put them on sticky notes on the side of my computer! [laughter]

That person may have moved from formula into principles: the principle of "I don't care!" [laughter]

Principles are different: they're *working ideas*, working laws, working theories about how things happen. Western esotericism (in particular, Western magic) has two schools: one which is very *formula* driven and one which is very *principle* driven. If you look at the *formula* driven, a very good example of that would be the Golden Dawn. The Golden Dawn methodology is very formula-driven. You are in *this*; you do *this*; you turn *here*; you turn *there*; now you layer this on top of it; now you add *this*. It has a very menu-like approach. And that's okay—that's a formula-approach.

But if we look at the writings of the Renaissance magi— such as Agrippa in his *Three Books of Occult Philosophy* or the so-called *Fourth Book* (which may or may not have been written by him) or we look at the writings of Ficino or Bruno—these are *principle-driven*. They give you *ideas* and *theories* that you actually have to spend some time with. What that means is that you have to internalize them and make them a part of yourself.

The problem with formula is that we expect formula to work in and of itself. "If I just do *this*, then *this* will happen." It's not necessarily so; we have to bring to it some of ourselves, we have to invest some of our own time and energy and resources into it—to the system of *principles*, which is what we're going to be talking about today. It involves that kind of investment of time.

The fact that you're all here and I can see what's on the desks leads me to know that you're all willing to do that, which is very good.

I want to give you a little background, because before we talk about any esoteric or philosophical system, it's important that you know its history. If you don't know its history, how are you going to know where it came from? If you don't know where it came from, how do you know if it's any good?

I was watching part of a documentary on yoga. They interview five yoga teachers at the beginning of the documentary. One said, "Oh, yoga's forty thousand years old" ... "Yoga's five thousand years old" ... "Yoga's two thousand years old" ... "I don't know how old yoga is, but I kind of think it's around four thousand years old, but I don't really care about that"...

How can you *teach* something if you don't care about where it came from? Because *they're not yoga teachers*. What they teach is calisthenics. [laughter] They're fitness instructors that wear expensive clothing and a turban, and like to chant in front of their brass "OM"! That's not yoga.

You have to have a sense of the history, because you are *part* of that chain. You are part of that—and until you *make* yourself a part of that, you're not going to really understand your relationship to what you're doing. You're not going to understand the sacrifices that took place in order to bring it to you—because, why should you? It's "just about me." Look, I just want to visualize my new car and get it over with! *I* need a job! (So does twenty percent of the population!) Hey, *I* need this! I need, I want.

That's not a good enough reason to move forward on the Path. You will get help in those things, definitely. But you have to move beyond them as end goals.

So part of that is understanding where your traditions have come from. We talk about Renaissance magic, and it's important to understand that according to Will Erich Peuckert (who was a Renaissance scholar): "The Renaissance is the rebirth of the occult sciences and not, as taught often in schools, the resurrection of classical philology and a forgotten vocabulary."

We think of the Renaissance as the "rebirth" of what we're going to be learning, and that's not it. If you look at what drove the Renaissance, it was originally Greek philosophy, but as soon as they found the *Corpus Hermeticum* and the Egyptian stuff, they said, "Oh, forget about that! Go translate *this*!" And that drove the Renaissance philosophically. That was it.

This happened because of incredible wealth. The cities of northern Italy, the urban population centers—particularly Venice, Milan, Florence, and Ferrara—had fantastic economic achievements, and they moved from being virtual communes into territorial states, exercising a regional influence across the Mediterranean. It was by the end of the Renaissance that territorial unification had taken place in France, Spain, and England, giving rise to these three very powerful empires in the modern era. It was through the wealth of these cities, and their princes and their bishops and their patrons of the merchant class, that the great achievements of the Renaissance took place in terms of art, in terms of science. Much of that was focused around Hermeticism and the great translations of the books that we have today.

It's very important to know that. This is the environment out of which these ideas came. People sought *more*. Who? *Wealthy* people sought more, because the peasant was too busy just trying to survive. That's usually the way it is. We tend to forget that because we don't live in that environment anymore.

It was during this period that we see a separation of the arts and sciences. Those begin to pull apart. We begin to *specialize*. It's not complete, by any stretch, but it's beginning. This separation would fully occur by the seventeenth century. The doctrines of the Roman Catholic Church were beginning to ebb slightly. It was still powerful, and dangerous to openly challenge, but its power to influence all these researches began to wane.

This in particular happened as a result of the Protestant Reformation and the full-blown warfare that would erupt across central Europe, particularly during the Thirty Years' War. They would be pre-occupied, and yet, oddly enough, despite this religious division, both sides—that is, the Protestants (composed of many, many groups) and the Catholics— would turn to Hermeticism as a possible unifying force, the thing that could possibly heal the gap.

Unfortunately, it did not.

Magic in the Renaissance is really the world of the imagination. In Paracelsus's credo, the first line is: "I am different— do not let this upset you." I've heard other translations: "I am different—do not be afraid." He was different. Magic did not disappear with the rise of the Roman Catholic Church; instead, it was adapted within it. Some of the prayers we just heard earlier are examples.

However, a *magical continuity* existed from the Mediterranean into Europe, albeit underground, through various magical texts. The *Greek Magical Papyræ* showed that thought and practice starting in late antiquity and moving into Europe in the twelfth century by way of Byzantium contained distinct unitary characteristics showing an uninterrupted period of theory and methods of magic.

That's very important, because this was done by the book. Things were written down, because that was the way it might be preserved—in case the person carrying the book ended up at a barbecue. Magic appears to have taken a turn in the Renaissance, moving away from many (what we think of as) "superstitious" operations of their medieval predecessors— from those things which you would see in the *Goetia* and in Solomonic magic into a kind of philosophic and natural magic. This natural magic is what gives rise to natural philosophy in the eighteenth century, which in turn gives rise to our modern scientific philosophy.

The necromancer of medieval lore is replaced with the philosopher, who sought to know and experience God directly and understand the laws of nature, as divine creation. That's very different from demanding obedience and servitude from beings, and being fearful of the world. In eighth century Europe, one probably *should* be afraid—it was a very different way of living.

Synesius of Cyrene (c. 370 to 413) was an archbishop and student of the martyred Neoplatonist Hypatia of Alexandria (d. 415). Synesius lay forth in his work *On Dreams* a theory of magic that was influential in Renaissance magical circles. He adopted the notion of the *pneuma*, or "spirit," from Greek philosophers. According to ancient tradition, the *pneuma* was a vaporous essence either *in* or *of* the blood that gives life to all animals, but also all *forms* of the material matrix upon which sensory and intellectual activity is formed.

This is the idea of a subtle anatomy, that this energy, this breath, circulates in us at all times, in and through us—and not just that, but it is a *part* of us: the blood. "Life is in the blood." I'm quoting Dracula's bug-eater! [laughter] "Life is in the blood." This vaporous essence becomes corporeal; it becomes dense.

This *pneuma* forms a kind of "sixth sense," the purpose or function of which is to codify information received from the senses so that they can be understood by the human intellect. It's a kind of medium—not just an energy, but rather a *translator* of things. For those in the Kabbalah, this would be identical with the *nephesh*, or the doctrine of the etheric body.

The language of "spirit" or the "soul" was seen in symbols— inner images or *phantasy*—and through imagination the intellect would make sense of the experiences of the world. **This phantasy, or inner world of the imagination, is said to be where the heavenly and material worlds unite.** To repeat: phantasy or the inner world of the imagination is where the heavenly and material worlds unite.

Our mind is not limited to just physical sensorium, nor is it exclusively in some kind of heavenly realm. "Heavenly" can be, in theory, outside of us or (as the Gospel says) within us. It is in our imagination where these things come together. That is the point. It is through a controlled and judicious use of our imagination that we can establish *harmony* between these outer and inner/objective and subjective realms of consciousness—and not just within ourselves, but in the universe as a whole.

Too often we think of our imagination as in Jungian therapy, where we just want to receive some kind of "harmonization" or "inner integration." But it isn't limited to *us*; it's within our mind and, of course, because things are inter-dependent, interconnected, it reaches out to the world as a whole. "As above, so below"; "as within, so without."

Professor Couliano was a professor of magic at the University of Chicago who was assassinated by the Romanian secret police in the late 1980s. As he wrote in his book: "Magic is not a factor of disorder. On the contrary, it is a means to establish or re-establish a peaceful co-existence between the consciousness and the unconscious where this co-existence is constantly under attack."[3] The purpose of all esoteric activities is to bring the unconscious into awareness. That is why we put so much emphasis on lucid dreaming, because when you dream you are fully immersed in your unconscious. Really what you're trying to do is become awake within your own unconscious. That's the purpose of this.

During this period you had a bizarre magical ecumenicism taking place. Greek, Egyptian, Roman texts were all looked at, as well as Arabic texts, and the co-called "Solomonic" or Judaeic texts. The most influential of these would be the *Radius*, the *Picatrix*, and the *Clavicula Solomonis*.

On the Rays was written by al-Kindi, who died in 873 CE. It stands out among the medieval magical literature for its sophistication. Its fundamental premise put forth that the universe is a continuous network of interlocking rays or

---

[3]Ioan Couliano (trans. Margaret Cook), *Eros and Magic in the Renaissance* (Chicago: University of Chicago Press, 1987) 126.

emanations from the planets and the four basic Elements of Earth, Air, Fire, and Water, and that these rays extend to the farthest reaches of the universe no matter what their source. They place us in a sea of vibrating energy with particular characteristics and tendencies. These rays then act and react upon one another according to their disposition—or, as al-Kindi calls it, their "hereditary nature." We could also call it "according to their *habituated* nature," the unconscious habits or instincts: what we call "karma." (We call karma *cause and effect*; the obscurations in our own mind, the confusion, is really just *habits*.)

In addition, human emotions such as joy, anger, sorrow, or love exert an invisible influence on the universe and other beings. We *consciously* exert this influence as well through the use of imagination, faith, and will. "Thus he is a microcosm and that explains why he receives, as does the world, power to induce by his own efforts movements within an equivalent substance, always provided that imagination, intention, and faith can be previously formed in the human soul." Or consciousness—within the human consciousness.

"This is because the spirit of imagination has *rays* or vibrations conforming to the world's rays. Thereby, too, they gain power to move by their own rays external things, just as the worlds—both higher, the spiritual, and the lower—stir rays of a thing according to the various moments and movements. When man conceives of a material thing through imagination, this thing acquires an actual existence according to the species in the imaginative powers."

So, when you *conceive* of a thing, *it exists*. When you think of something, it exists—even if for that brief moment within your own mind. If you conceive it powerfully and strongly, it exists longer in your mind. If you conceive of it in your mind strongly enough, long enough, then it will exist in an outer objective sense as well. Which is wonderful—this is why, in the *Corpus Hermeticum*, it says: "Think of me and I am there." Just by thinking of me, *I am there*. That's why illumination and salvation aren't some distant point, but are *right now*. Think of it—but, you see, you don't hold on to it. You don't *believe* it; you have to believe it, and hold on to it. You have to hold on to it.

What we do: our minds wander. In alchemical manuscripts, they show a rabbit—in the East, they call it the "monkey mind"; here, it's a rabbit.

[Audience Member: Drifting.]

Drifting. That's our mind. We have to still it, make it still.

[Audience Member: When you say that, I think immediately about the practical application of it. Can you talk about it in terms of the meditation that you took us through, and *effective* imagining?]

As soon as you think of a painting, it exists. As soon as you think of it, it exists. It doesn't pop on the wall, fully formed, like some spiritualist phenomena—but it exists. You then bring it into being depending on how much focus you give to that idea. When we think of ideas like joy and compassion, or love and happiness, they're not in an abstract sense, but in a very real sense. Providence. What makes one person happy may not make another person happy; but if we're looking for genuine happiness, then there's different things along the way.

It's wonderful for us to be thinking about spiritual ideas and abstractions, but some time around one-o'clock what would *really* make us happy is for me to shut up and for us to have some soup! [laughter] We think about things, and we give them energy. First it's a thought, an abstraction; but then it goes from just a thought to a very visceral *feeling*. "Look, I'm really, really *hungry!*"

You recall times when you've gotten very frustrated because you're just *way*-tired, or -hungry, or -(fill-in-the-blank)? Now, if you *stay* in that state, different things will happen. Either someone will say, "Here's a hamburger, already!" Or, people get irritated with you—but it moves *out* from just being within you to the environment around you. If you do it in a more controlled and conscious manner—in a more focused and open manner—you can focus on that thing you want to do or accomplish, and it radiates out. Then you get that phone call from someone you haven't heard from in five years who says: "Hey, I'm working on [blah-blah], would you like to help me out?" Yeah! Very nice! Nice synchronicity, or whatever you want to call it; coincidence.

As we hold on to something in our mind, we create it. Then we create it and give it a kind of life or energetic quality based upon the *emotions*. The problem is that, with us, our emotions are often *confused*. Instead of having joyful and harmonious emotions—because, why is the friend you haven't heard from in five years going to call you to help him with a project if you're not really radiating out a general joyfulness? A way to help them as well? You're helping open up those links and those channels, those connections to others. In return, it comes back to you.

It can be just that people are *nicer* to you, and that you're nicer to others! It happens a whole bunch of different ways on a practical level, it doesn't just have to be with "stuff." But it's in how we relate to one another, how we get along. It all depends on what we hold in our mind—and what we hold in our mind is what we *want*. It's what we desire; it's what we think is going to make us happy. Sometimes it does, sometimes it doesn't.

[Audience Member: Remember the rules of the Path. Wrapping that energy, that vibration, using that hypnotic rhythm. You start getting that will back on track and, finally, the vibrations of Nature pick up what you're doing and put momentum behind it, *if* you hold it long enough. If you *don't* hold it long enough, that same momentum will just dissipate out in all directions and keep you in that drifting or dissipative mode. So even though I'm feeling antsy about eating, and I'm getting really uptight, it doesn't have to be just some kind of "glorious" feeling that you can ramp up to project out onto something and hold good thoughts, I can take that "not such a good" feeling—*still* a very strong vibration—and let it ramp up higher and higher until I just go: "Man, I've gotta get something to eat!" Or I could notice that, hey, that vibration is making me feel this way, but this is just a visceral sensation of a *vibration* that's actually very powerful. That's why all these other techniques that we artificially induce are done: to put us in a place of high vibration. So the fasting, the abstinence, all of these things that we've gone through—you may be so well-along on the Path, I hope, that you kind of get into this "blissful, bubble-head" state where everything's going smooth, you don't really have to do much of anything, you get into this flow, and—it's nice, but, how do you ramp up your energy at that point? You don't have the little things that happen during the day that annoy you. Or excite you, even. We all know people like that, who've got everything going for them and they can't get excited about anything! Right? And they're just kind of in *neutral.* So, as practition-ers, what we do a lot of times is use these artificial states to ramp our energy up. Nobody in here can tell me honestly it's "fun" to fast! Nobody can tell me it's fun to be abstinent from anything that you desire or like! We put ourselves in those artificial situations in order to create this "hyper-vibration."]

Essentially, you're looking for emotional intensity, but the emotional intensity that we often use is of the most-controlled, habituated nature. It's stationary. It's not one which we're aware of, and by consciously working with our relationship with others, and all beings on all levels (as in the meditation we did earlier), we're consciously generating what we consider to be the most important emotion of all, which is genuine compassion, and a desire that we are happy and that others are happy, and that these are okay. Not only that, but the things which make us happy don't necessarily have to be "great, philosophical, enlightened ideals."

There's different levels of happiness for the moment. Some of them are very mundane and transitory—and that's okay.

Others are, of course, more complicated and more sophisticated. For example: "I need to have something to eat," that's good. "I need to have a place to live." But now I also have to focus—with that taken care of, what's next? That's when we talk about *self-realization*. Again, not getting too caught up in our own self-realization, but having a constant feedback going, because these rays, as we call them, are going out; these thoughts are constantly emanating out and crossing over one another. Their impact in life are like strings on an instrument.

[Audience Member: So is it contemplating what we're focusing on more intensely? Bringing awareness to that? Because if we "think" we want something, and our emotional intensity is really not focused on that, then it's not going to happen.]

Yes, that's right. You get whatever your emotional intensity is [focused on]. That's why we have to talk about (at some point, not necessarily today) why the nature of understanding your own mind is so important and why most esoteric systems in the west that I'm familiar with fail pretty miserably in helping people to understand the nature of their own mind, which is pretty ironic. That's why Regardie had that whole, big section in the beginning of *The Golden Dawn* about why you should undertake psychotherapy before you do this—and that's a section that most people ignore. They bring their own "stuff" to the practice, and all that does is magnify it and bring it out, and that's why these groups explode. They're not working on actually understanding their own neurotic tendencies.

Your neurotic tendencies are the source of all of your unhappiness. Recognizing them and then just letting them go—like Jesus said to the woman: "Just sin no more." What is sin? It is error. Just don't do it anymore! Recognize it, and then don't do it. Simply by not doing it you bring an end to that habit.

We don't possess a subconscious mind—we *are* a subconscious. Almost everything that happens is below our threshold of awakening. All of public relations and marketing is based on this; I know that well, I tell my students that. We have to understand that, too. *You* are the only one who can understand your own mind, and these are the things we're going over that you have to understand: that your mind is *powerful*. Parts of your mind are extremely, emotionally powerful; they are emotions, they're not rational. Because it's so powerful, and emotion is the most powerful thing, we need the most powerful emotion there is which would be the best for all of us: which is *compassion*.

Otherwise, there will always be division. Division will always keep us in duality. Duality will always keep us in suffering and in misery, in a state of "fallen grace" or "sin," or error.

Now we need to move on.

The power of imagination is the ability to embody ideas, emotions, and concepts in an orderable construct. Once done, this image or controlled fantasy can be produced with such strength and clarity that it takes on a life or momentum of its own. The only thing which can either add or detract from it actually manifesting materially at this point is the faith or confidence of the magician.

For al-Kindi, magic was wholly dependent upon the operator. If the imagination is sufficiently developed and directed with confidence and faith, then the operations have a high probability of success, as the laws of nature are on their side.

In *Religion and the Decline of Magic*, Keith Thomas describes the difference between "magic" and "petitionary prayers" as such.

> The essential difference between the prayers of a churchmen and the spells of a magician was that only the latter claimed to work automatically. A prayer had no certainty of success and would not be granted if God chose not to concede it. A spell, on

the other hand, need never go wrong, unless some
detail or ritual observation had been omitted or a
rival magician had been practicing stronger counter-
magic.[4]

A prayer, in other words, was a form of supplication; a spell
was a mechanical means of manipulation. Magical acts can
also be carried out or reinforced through sounds and other
actions. We here quote from al-Kindi:

> There are indeed speeches which, coming forth from
> the mouth of man, while expressing imagination,
> faith, and desire, actualize in the world motions
> within individualized beings.[5]

There are sounds and colors, again, what to they do? They
reach deep inside you. They go past your objective, rational
mind—as Mike said last night so wonderfully: "There are
some things that just draw our attention." [laughter] That's
right. What are those things "hooking into"? Our feelings,
our imaginative part—which is our psychic mind, our unconscious.

Sound produced in actions emit rays like everything else
in action, and through their rays in the world, work upon the
elements, similarly to other beings.

These sounds or *phonæ* are the magical language. This is
also known as the *natural language*. The symbols that come
to us are important, because we're going to be talking almost
exclusively about what we call the "Element of Air," and
understanding the language of symbols, the "language of the
birds," or the "green language." Birds are symbolic of different
states of spiritual awakening; it was a dove that descended
upon Jesus during his baptism. The dove is a symbol of the

---

[4]Keith Thomas, *Religion and the Decline of Magic* (New York:
Charles Scribner's Sons, 1971) 41.

[5]Quoted in Couliano, *Eros and Magic, op. cit.*, 121.

Holy Spirit, and the "Holy Spirit" means the Holy *Creative* Spirit—the Spirit of Awakening. It is that holy energy, that creative energy, that awakens us; it's a *creative* power that is present in the world. It's identical with the kabbalistic notion of *Shekhinah*. It's *present, here*; it *awakens* here. It motivates, it brings things to life. That's why it's the Holy Spirit that allows for the impregnation of Mary. The creative energy is *everywhere*.

The *Key of Solomon* is one of the most famous magical texts. We see a lot of use of Solomonic magic in the seventeenth century. We see a lot of inclusion of Kabbalah, so we see Kabbalah moving away from strictly what we call "Jewish Kabbalah" (which is redundant, Kabbalah is, by its nature, Jewish) into a kind of "Hermetic" Kabbalah. Actually, first it is a kind of "Christianized" Kabbalah, where a lot of Christian mystics saw Kabbalah within the Holy Upper Trinity a way of justifying the Holy Trinity. We see that way of looking back, saying, "Here's this Jewish mysticism; this is in support of our esoteric doctrines—they're not really heretical at all." They project upon it a lot of Christian ideas.

It moves forward from there into what we think of as a "Hermetic" Kabbalah now. This Hermetic Kabbalah includes not just strictly Jewish ideas but also Christian ideas and ideas taken from the classical Mediterranean world (what we would call "pagan" or "pre-Christian" classical civilizations). So there's more and more layering of ideas and symbols onto it.

Kabbalah also includes at this point a great deal of astrology and begins to include, at later points, alchemy. We see this transformation of ideas, and that's very important, because ideas transform and grow, too. Sometimes they do it well and sometimes they do it poorly—but they move forward. Traditions are rarely dropped down "full form."

[Audience Member: This is the seventeenth century?]

No, no; this is much earlier. Probably—well, the word "Kabbalah" isn't really used until about the tenth century,

but there are earlier mystical practices that it's based on. By
about the twelfth century, you begin to see the emergence
of the Christian Kabbalah. The Hermetic Kabbalah evolves
around the fourteenth century.

One of the most interesting points about Kabbalah is the
use of Divine Names—again, the magical sounds or *phona*.
We also get at this point so-called magical alphabets, of which
Hebrew is considered one. We have many that get revealed
at different times.

The purpose of Kabbalah, of meditations and prayers, is
very straightforward, as Scholem points out. It is to create
a condition where the spiritual world reveals itself to the
kabbalist, to the man's prayer, and that this mystical revelation furthers the individual's harmony with God and, of
course, with his fellow human beings. The end point of all
this is absorption into the Godhead—whatever that means. It
seems to mean different things to different people. At times,
it is often described as a kind of "negative enlightenment,"
like you see in Hinayana Buddhism, where the person is just
absorbed back into the Godhead, the person is absorbed
into Nirvana and ceases to exist anymore. Sometimes it's
described as that. Sometimes it's described as something else:
as a *full awakening* of their powers. The Godhead is a full
potential and possibility.

We have, of course, the Italians, of which Marsilio Ficino
was the most important, and Pico della Mirandola (one of
my favorites), whom we quote: "Nature performs in a natural
way the things that a magician achieves by his Art." That is
the same as the alchemical statement: "The alchemist is the
handmaid of Nature." The alchemist "speeds up" the natural
process.

"Speeds up" the process—does not "circumvent" it, does
not "go around" it. Speeds it up.

Among the Germans—and this is the fifteenth century,
into the early sixteenth—we have Johannes Reuchlin. His
book *The Miraculous Word* became a sort of Bible of early

Christian Kabbalah. It is from that that he claims to have reconstructed the true Name of Jesus in Hebrew, taking the Tetragrammaton (the four-lettered Name of God) Yod-Heh-Vav-Heh (יהוה) and inserting the letter "shin" (ש) as the middle letter, giving us Yod-Heh-Shin-Vav-Heh (יהשוה). We see this used continuously from then in various esoteric circles, practices, and meditations.

The main subject of Reuchlin's first book on Kabbalah, *The Miraculous Word* (or *Name*) was to expose the miraculous powers of the hidden, divine Name—the Pentagrammaton—formed from the insertion of the letter "shin" into the middle of the Tetragrammaton. This name formed, according to Reuchlin and his source Pico della Mirandola, the secret Name of Jesus. Notice it's a "secret" Name; we're always looking for "secret" Names.

In the Jewish Kabbalah, we can find formation of Divine Names that cannot be detected in classical texts which are as bizarre as this form of Yeheshua that we see. For those of you familiar with French esotericism as we approach the period of Christmas within various Martinist orders and groups, this is the time of the year when they perform a ritual known as the "Yeheshua Ceremony," in which they use the Pentagrammaton to pull light down into their heart. A wonderful ritual to see.

Reuchlin would also write another book called *The Art of Kabbalah*, and this became the Bible of Christian Kabbalah after its publication. He dedicated it to Pope Leo X, who had an interest in Pythagoreanism. The basic style of the *Art* was that of a dialogue between a Pythagorean Muslim that is mediated by a Jew, who explains how Kabbalah contains the oldest Divine Wisdom.

[Audience Member: How does *that* work?]

Well, you see, Reuchlin got called before a council... [laughter] But, he got these texts because the Grand Inquisitor came to Mainz. Emperor Maximilian I had ordered that all books in Hebrew be burnt on August 15, 1509. However, authorities had asked Reuchlin what might be useful, because Reuch-

lin read Hebrew. He thought it might have been a trap for
his Jewish-leaning sympathies, so he had to defend himself
against charges of heresy. Fortunately, Reuchlin was an incredibly well-off man and representatives from fifty-three towns
in Swabia spoke on his behalf (of course, putting themselves
in danger in doing so). In thankfulness for the risk, the rabbis
of the town supplied him with the documents which would
become *The Art of Kabbalah.*

We also have other books: the *Sefer ha-Raziel* (the *Book
of Raziel*), the *Fifty Gates of Wisdom*—of which was said the
King and Magus Solomon himself was only able to penetrate
to the forty-ninth of these Gates.

We have Johannes Trithemius and his writings—the Abbot of Sponheim. He would influence the writings of Dr. John
Dee—and, yes, Trithemius *also* attracted the attention of
Maximilian I! [laughter] No surprise there, right? But he is
most famous for having tutored Agrippa, whom they called
the Prince of Magicians, the author of *Three Books of Occult Philosophy.* Agrippa supposedly wrote this book at the
tender age of twenty-two. He was a contemporary of Paracelsus. Some believe that he did not write the book, but that
Trithemius did, and Agrippa was told to publish it (which
took a while—ten to twenty years after it was originally
written, it came out).

We also have, in the sixteenth century, Jacob Boehme. He
was born in Silesia. There is a story how, as a very young boy,
he was working to be a cobbler, and an incredibly old man
calls him out, yelling: "Jacob! Jacob!" He gets up and walks
out, and the old man tells him that: "You are blessed among
all beings and will be great. You will have many profound
revelations." Of course, the young boy runs away, scared.
Later on, Jacob Boehme was a cobbler, a shoemaker, and he
has spontaneous visions. Some of these would occur on light
reflecting off a spoon, a mirror, a glass. He would have these
profound philosophical visions.

His writings were *very* important; his visions were very

important. Many of his early English followers—known as "Behmenists"—were later absorbed into the Quaker movement.

Among the English we have Robert Fludd. One of his famous puns is:

> For what we do presage is not in gross,
> For we be brethren of the Rosie Cross:
> We have the Mason's Word and the second sight,
> Things for to come we can fortell aright.

Here we have a reference to what we call the "Rosicrucians" or the "Rosy Cross." It is Fludd who wrote *A Complete Apology for the Fraternity of the Rosy Cross* in 1616. It is the Rosicrucian movement which we will not go into at this point—but maybe later on in the future—that becomes one of the main focal points for Western esotericism.

We also have John Dee, whom you are somewhat familiar with, and others.

When we talk about *The Magus*—and I like this, this is really one of my favorite books—"in him, God and Nature meet." Sartorius von Walterhausen. It's not just an inner state of nature—what we think of as "the whole world"—they *meet* in the magus. For me, for my great-uncle, and for others I know, maybe one of the best expressions of this is a poem by Johann Scheffler (1624-1677). He wrote under the pen name "Angelus Silesius," the Angel of Silesia.

> I know that without me
> God can no moment live
> Were I to die
> Then He could no longer survive.
> I am as great as God,

And He is small like me.
He cannot be above,
Nor I below him be.
In me God is Fire,
And I in Him its glow,
In common is our life,
Apart we cannot grow.
He is God-in-Man to me,
To Him I am both indeed.
His thirst I satisfy
He helps me in my need.
God is such as He is,
I am what I must be.
If you know one, in truth,
You know both Him and me.
I am the vine which he doth plant and cherish most.
The fruit which grows from me is God the Holy
Ghost.[6]

This is where we see a movement away—if we look at esoteric traditions, we see this progression. I talked a little bit about this in *Kabbalah for Health & Wellness* where I discussed the three aspects of a practitioner of the occult, the occultists or magi. One function is that of *healing*, that is, genuine healing of others. One is that they are a kind of "moral prophet," not so much to make prophecies and predictions, but to *see things as they are*, and to make statements about that. Another is that they function as a *priest*; there is a priestly function, which is a unitive function.

That is what we have within us; those are the different qualities that we are bringing forth, these different, if you will, "job descriptions." With that, we have the introduction of what we call "theurgy," which means "god-making." We

---

[6]Quoted in Christopher Bilardi, *The Red Church, or the Art of Pennsylvania German Braucherei* (Los Angeles: Pendraig Publishing, 2009) 99.

really look at this on a practical level, though, because the definition changes from the classical notion of theurgy—it changes a little bit. It's Greek. The "god-making" is within ourselves.

So the theurgist is not just a "magician" moving things around, talking to disincarnate beings or casting spells for hire; nor are they just a mystic, absorbed in their own navel-gazing contemplations. They are *both*. They are very active and dynamic beings, able to take those profound, inner states and make them meaningful, to guide their actions so they act with awareness, they act with illumination, they act with Light—enlightenment, illumination. That theurgic notion was the highest ideal.

That brings us to a good one:

> The magician operates in a manner wholly different from that of his precursors [that is, the Renaissance magicians]. Where the one had a direct line to the God or the gods of his tribe, the other [the Renaissance magus] works with different techniques, different contexts. It is always seeking to break through into the inner realm itself, to speak directly to God as his ancestor, the tribal shaman, had once been able to do. Thus his magic is a practical extension of a philosophical/mystical underpinning, and without taking this into account, his dream of unity (however partial or superficial) with deity is to mistake his whole purpose.[7]

That is important, because when we look at the operations that we're going to do today—which are from the *Three*

---

[7]Caitlín and John Matthews, *Walkers Between the Worlds: The Western Mysteries from Shaman to Magus* (Rochester, VT: Inner Traditions, 2004).

Books of Occult Philosophy—when we look at magic, we have different levels. We have *folk magic*, which is often superstitious. It's superstitious because, like a monkey, it imitates things without knowing why, hoping to get results.

Then we have the same thing being done by someone who is a magician, but they're just trying to move things around. They just want to "pull the levers of the cosmos," if you will. There's no greater ambition than the action and the results of the action itself.

Then we have this magus, for whom this is all true and good, but there is a *great* philosophical underpinning. It's not just so that I can pull the levers of the universe—but *why?* Why does the universe give back this way? What is my place in it? What is the *end result* of this? Their philosophy is one of "enlightenment," "illumination."

The *Three Books of Occult Philosophy* are, again, one of the central teachings in Western magic. You find them everywhere. Very few people have actually read them. I do understand that there is a new translation out, from the Latin, by people who actually can translate Latin and are magicians. The magic described in the *Three Books* is of three natures. Book One covers *natural magic.* By "natural magic," we're referring to the elements in successful magical operations. Magic, at this point, also includes what we would consider "general physics and chemistry." What we think of as "physics and chemistry" would be considered part of natural magic.

Book Two is *celestial magic.* This deals primarily with planetary magic, planetary symbols, magic squares, with an emphasis on Kabbalah and the Hebrew alphabet in magical acts.

The third book is *ceremonial magic.* This is the key to all of Agrippa's writings, and it is the most important book. In fact, this is probably the one you're supposed to read first; it was very common to put these things out of order in these old texts. Only if you make it to the Third Book do you understand what is essential for a successful operation.

Then, of course, we have the *Fourth Book*, or "pseudo-Agrippa," which contains a summary of all magical information or requirements, the *Heptameron*, as well as other books that are of use that we will talk about at some other time.

✳ ✳ ✳

Shem HaMephorash Seal

◇ PART TWO ◇

I once did a magical ritual in Italy for a group of academics—
who will remain nameless! Some of these names you've all
heard. [laughter] It was wonderful to see the response after-
wards. It was wonderful.

That "Golden Thread," of course, you say you have trouble
tracing it. That's because—and who was it I was speaking
to last night? Someone had asked me about "esotericism
and culture and community," and what is my relationship to
it—did I grow up in an environment where occult ideas were
part of the community function?

I said no, because you rarely have that. When you look
at the Golden Thread, what you're seeing is esoteric ideas
constantly adapting themselves to the external world. That's
what makes esotericism unique, because, in fact, there really
is—let me repeat that. When we look at the esoteric thread
or current as it moves across the Mediterranean and into
Europe, Western esotericism is constantly adapting itself to
the outer world. You don't see that in Asia; so, the whole
notion of esotericism is really unique to the West.

Of course, these are Greek words that we're using. Not
Sanskrit, not Chinese—they're Greek: "outer" and "inner."
"Outer" teaching—which is the Church, within which is said
there is no other teaching. Now, they don't *call* themselves
an "exoteric" teaching—that's how *we* perceive them. That's
very important. Things shift around; it's a matter of power-
perception, for most teachings.

Judaism would be an example. There you had esoteric
teachings, people knew about them, they knew who the rabbis
were that were teaching them. You may or may not have

been encouraged to go to them at different times, because of
the historical events that unfolded around them—but they
certainly weren't *hidden*. It was just: "Okay, well, you know,
if you want to go do that! Go ahead."

Whereas in the dominantly Roman Catholic and then later
Protestant culture of Europe, for all the great benefits that
it brought to Europe, at the same time, one of the downsides
was that some time after the tenth century—when you see
Christianity moving throughout Europe and Northern Europe
in particular, up to the fourth through the tenth centuries—
you could get away with *anything* as long as you put "in the
name of the Father, of the Son, and of the Holy Ghost" after
it. [laughter] Which is *great*, because that's what we're going
to be doing this afternoon! [laughter]

As things change, as things codify and get more rigid,
you see people saying, "No! *This* is the way it is!" But that's
duality. They're not looking at things progressively.

Originally, the notion of inward reflection and peace is
wonderful. That's missing in a lot of churches. The great
ritual liturgy of the Roman Catholic Church, or some of its
Protestant offshoots (the Anglican Church or the Lutheran
Church)—these are wonderful liturgies that *elevate* you. You
feel *specialness*, particularly the use of saints. "That one is
like *me*—I can identify with him." The chain. There's a reason
why within Catholic Europe that the saints had greater call
at times as local deities than the main church itself.

Agrippa says prayers to the saints are very powerful because they are like us and hear our calls. Maybe that's not
necessarily true, but it shows an understanding of this idea
of abstraction and distance that many people actually feel
with the Church's teachings. Because those higher teachings
are too abstract for day-to-day life. That's where we get
into these navel-gazers, who just can't connect to reality.
You know them—you used to call them the "New Age bliss
bunnies" and all that. [laughter]

Terra firma! Put the feet on the ground! You don't see

that kind of stuff in Jewish mysticism. Jewish mysticism has strong warnings about that kind of thing, because it was part of the culture. Again, at different times and places, it was not supported, but people knew it existed. It didn't go away; it wasn't pushed out, except by historical social pressures, rather than theological ones.

In the East, everyone knew that being a yogi was the one way you could free yourself from the caste system. You were then free. In China, in Tibet—and I'm sure in other places as well that I'm unfamiliar with—temple worship, daily worship, you want to study with the lama? Fine. You want to go to the hermitage? Fine. You want to go study with the yogi? Fine. They all knew where they were. If they didn't know where they were, they knew how to get a hold of them—"I'll talk to *this* one, they'll know!"

So the relationship was there. It wasn't hidden. They may have hid themselves because they didn't want to be bothered, but it was not hidden. That's the difference: Western esotericism becomes *occultism*, or *hidden*. Hidden for its own survival.

Unfortunately, in the modern era, many people like to *keep* it hidden, in the sense that they're "protecting" the teachings. They're not. The teachings don't need to be "protected." They're *self-protected*. To this I like to quote His Holiness Dudjom Rinpoche, head of the Nyingma order when it was first in exile: "All these teachings are self-protected—because either you can do it or you can't. And either you have the wherewithal to *learn* how to do it or you don't."

We don't need to protect them; we just need to preserve them and transmit them. The same thing in Western esotericism, we saw this whole notion of "protection" even in the twentieth century, particularly in the last thirty years. Not so much now, from, say, the eighties to the nineties, into around 2000. There were a lot of folks saying, "We've got to protect this!" What you're doing is you're protecting your own ignorance. You're protecting your own ignorance from people not knowing as much as you think you do. [laughter]

What had happened is that means of transmission built up, and this Golden Thread was one of small, informal groups. Think about that: small, informal groups—smaller than this—would need to trade books, copy them by hand, talk about what they did, write things down, and pass it on to another generation, or to someone else. This is how it kept moving, how it kept alive. Then small groups might form more informally, such as John Dee's "School of the Night," where these people would get together to talk about things. It wasn't just what *we* think of as occultism; it covered that whole area, the first book of Natural Magic—what we consider science and mathematics—as well.

We move forward into the early part of the eighteenth century. In the eighteenth century you have Freemasonry becoming a more present force. Then you have the formation of the first Grand Lodge, meaning that several lodges got together and recognized the authority of a superior administrative body over them, so they could have a uniform practice. For reasons that no one's sure of, Freemasonry takes off. Within thirty years you have *all* of these lodges in Europe. They existed before, but now there's all these rituals and rites, and by the middle of the eighteenth century you have this full-blown thing you call "Scottish Rite."

What happened at this time, is that Masonry—now a very symbolic organization—went from being operative stonemasons to using the symbols of operative stonemasonry in a philosophical sense. They became "speculative masons." But they had to have *something*, because why would these rich guys want to sit in lodge with these stonemasons if they didn't *know* something?

Well, what they knew was most likely *geometry*—it's probably no more sophisticated than that. But what is geometry? It's the Queen of the Sciences. Without it, nothing happens. All of this is because of geometry. So it's very important—they knew *math*.

There was a time when math was considered an occult art that you couldn't study. They knew math, they knew algebra, they knew geometry—they could read and write. Think about that. That's a *lot*. They traveled freely from country to country, and met with other people.

This became an organization that many believe was co-opted by secret societies. I think to some degree, that's true—but in an *informal* way. I don't think it was a big, conspiratorial thing—I think it was an opportunity, and here was a conduit. Let's use it.

By the middle of the eighteenth century, you have these Masonic Rites which are incredibly Hermetic, chivalric, es-oteric, alchemical, just popping up like mushrooms all over France and Germany, to some degree England. For some reason they didn't take on to the appended rites as much. But, just all over the place—and why is that? Because people wanted *secret knowledge*, and just like then, for every seller of a secret, there's a buyer. [laughter]

We know that too well, don't we?

[Audience Member: We're here!] [laughter]

So! [laughter] I'm not selling you snake oil! [laughter] But that's the point! You've all been through the mill—and you're better off for it, right? You still get tempted back every now and then. That's okay.

With that, a lot of groups came up. Different societies—secret societies—would form as a side group (not just in Masonry, but in other structures and social settings). They'd say: "You *know* something—you have an interest. You might want to talk to 'this' person over here, or to 'this' one..." It becomes a recruiting ground. Sometimes, that recruit-ing ground is very open—such as when Pasqualez does his overgrown Elus Cohens (or "Elect Cohens": Elect Priests). Pasqualez—who was a semi-literate Portuguese Jew using a phoney Masonic warrant to establish his quasi-Masonic magical body in France in the 1850s—was a *dynamic* guy. He couldn't speak French all that well, but he'd get these aristocrats around him because he had a *magical system*—an *operative* system—and it was very detailed and difficult, with rituals that could last maybe six or seven hours.

Much of it, though, was very devotional and very Roman Catholic. That surprises a lot of students today when they read it—they're surprised. Why is it so Roman Catholic? Well—he's in Europe in the eighteenth century! What *else* is it going to be? That's neither right nor wrong; it's just the model of expression that he used, because the rituals he used were often from the earlier grimoires, the Solomonic texts. They were variations of those.

His lodges were very in the open, but when they collapsed, the degrees got absorbed into the higher degrees of Scottish Rite. Not a lot of Scottish Rite Masons know that they have the operative rites of the Elus Cohens in the twenty-fifth or twenty-eighth degree or whatever—they don't. But the *seeds* of it are there. The pieces of it, like a file, waiting to be opened on a computer.

So that's what each of those degrees began to represent: little files that could be opened. You had these side orders, then, that would be fully expressed on their own: "We no longer recruit just Masons—we're open to everyone." These orders ebb and flow, they come and go. Sometimes the tradition is down to a few people.

When the Martinist Order was established in Paris in the late-nineteenth century, there were *two people*, and what they had was hardly a "tradition." They had a few symbols that they had inherited, they had some words and some vague means of recognition. They recognized each other as having come from this distant lineage.

Other times it's more complete, more whole. Some of those traditions came to the United States, of course, during the late-seventeenth century when Johannes Kelpius went to the Wissahickon in Fairmount Park—which at that point was wilderness. If I understand correctly, a lot of people avoided it because of the rattlesnakes. There, he and a bunch of hermits calling themselves the "Women in the Wilderness," after the Book of Revelation, contemplated a lot of theosophical and Behmenist teachings, those of Jacob Boehme and others, and Kabbalah and alchemy. They spent their time waiting for the Second Coming.

A fellow would follow after him known as Conrad Beissel. Beissel would arrive too late; Kelpius would be dead. Beissel would make his way to Ephrata and establish the Ephrata community there. It would evolve and change every time. It would have lay members who were married and had families who would come. It had celibate males and celibate females: the Brotherhood of Sion and the Sisterhood of the Rose of Sharon. Even within there you would have people rise up who would have an almost saintly nature—Beissel himself was profoundly, *profoundly* charismatic. Despite his frail, sickly appearance, the chicks couldn't get enough of him! [laughter]

[Audience Member: Like Rasputin?]

No! Because you see, Rasputin, at least, *indulged*! [laughter] I think for Conrad, I think it was...well, just kind of "seeping out of his pores"! [laughter] So—that might have been part of the attraction! The unattainable. We know how that works for all of us.

But he was a *profoundly* charismatic person; he was profoundly *visionary*. In his descriptions of his visions, if you know how to read the language, they're just like out-of-body experiences that would last for *days*. Then he'd come back and tell what he had seen. Not unlike Hildegard von Bingen. They thought she was dead many times, and then she'd wake up. Glad they didn't start doing the embalming process... [laughter]

That *charisma* was his *magia*, his magic. He went off at one point because things were going wrong, and he went to see one of the last survivors of the Kelpius community, who was a hermit known as Matthias—I think it was Conrad Matthias. Conrad is looked upon by some as a "saint" of great magical renown that is sometimes used as a focal point of aspiration in some pow-wow circles.

Now, the word *pow-wow* we don't know the origin or meaning of, but in practice it is the survival of medieval and Renaissance magic—particularly Northern Hermeticism or German magic—in the Colonial Period to the present. It is very different from what many of you would have encountered.

That said, within the traditional structures of, say, the Elus Cohens, a very formal, ritualized magical order, within the written text of Agrippa, within the very informal and fragmented teachings that exist in different circles in the Pennsylvania German community (or what's left of it), parts of Ohio, streaming down into Kentucky and West Virginia—and really those influences are *not* Scotch and Irish, they are actually traceable to the earlier German lineages that moved through—down into the Carolinas and even further south into New Orleans, even moving into Hoodoo, we see several key things always occurring. So, between these very diverse and divergent streams of practice—from simple old ladies healing warts to magicians drawing circle on the floor for rituals that last six hours at a pop, invoking all sorts of angelic beings—we see *four common texts* beings used.

These four biblical books play a critical role in Western magical practices: the Book of Genesis, the Psalms, the Gospel of John, and the Revelation of John (or the Apocalypse). You will note that Agrippa says when creating your "magic book," the first thing you must do is you must draw upon the first page the symbol of one of the scenes from the Revelation of John, and on the last page you must draw a scene from the Revelation of John. The first page is Jesus with the sword in the mouth; the last page is the lamb upon the Book of the Seven Seals.

These four books are *critical.* You've *got* to grasp that.

It is often stated that "the wages of sin are death." The reason Genesis is important is because it provides us with the origins and the fall of man. In Christian tradition, suffering, sickness, and death are the result of sin. Sin may be the

Original Sin or what we call the "Fall from Grace," and "grace" is the Edenic state or state of perfection. This in many ways can be looked upon as the "Golden Age." We've talked about the Four Ages: the Golden Age, the Silver Age, the Bronze Age, and, now, the Age of Iron—what is called by the Hindus and in Vajrayāna the Kali Yuga, the age of suffering and death. These four ages are what they use as the progression of society, of humanity. They are cyclic—they're constantly re-occurring.

That means the key point is *creation is an on-going state*, it's not a simple "one-point" deal. It happens continuously. This is very difficult to grasp.

So, we fall from grace—we could think of it as a fall from a "unitive state" or "non-duality." The fall was into *duality*, either-or. One of the things I'd recommend to—because we may not have time to go over it—is that it's really important that you understand some of the writings around Isaac Luria, since Luria and the Kabbalah forms in many ways the core parts of Western magic. In his book *Windows of the Soul*—the one that's readable—this is talked about quite a bit. There are four attempts at Creation. It's doesn't just "happen." "Oh, tried that—didn't quite work...tried *that*—didn't quite work worse..." It's interesting to find again this number *four*, these four phases.

We finally get to where we are now and, of course, it's considered a poor imitation of the first effort—kind of like a photocopy of a photocopy of a photocopy. So *sin* is to *miss the point*; it's to be in *error*. And where does the error take place? *In the mind*.

That's the only place it *can* take place. That's very important to know.

Suffering, sickness, and death are the result of sin; they're the result of the error of the mind, the error of our thinking and then the actions that follow forth from that. So when we accept Christ into our lives, after the Second Coming, the faithful of the dead will be resurrected, and suffering, sickness, and death will be no more.

But this depends on who you ask. The *outer* notion is that there is some kind of eternal physical life on Earth in this "golden state" because they're looking at it as static—everything's linear, not cyclic. If you look at it from a different view, what we're talking about is your illumination. Duality is no longer an issue for you. We call that *enlightenment* or *salvation*. That means that death is no more, because there can be no more error.

If you understand cause and effect, the effects of your actions, then you not only *wouldn't*, but why *would* you do anything that would be harmful to you? That means there's no more illness, no more suffering, no more death—you are filled with *light*, you are *awake*. This is the "awakening of the dead," the resurrection of the dead. They talk about Mary as being "asleep," and we "go to sleep in the Lord." Asleep to be *awakened*.

[Audience Member: Then spirituality does become an individual decision.]

It's *always* individual, because no one can do the work for you. We *help* each other, we learn from one another, we speed up the learning curve, and by creating environments that are conducive to us speeding up the learning curve—

[Audience Member: We realize it's in our best interest.]

That's exactly it! Really, it's in my best interest.

[Audience Member: There's less negativity that you bounce off.]

Exactly. If you want to be selfish about it, it's in my best interest to help. To put it in the most selfish terms, it's *still* in your best interest.

It's interesting to view this, because Gnosticism as well as some schools of Vajrayāna Buddhism really see material life as an *error*—a mistake has been made. You're not in that "archetypal" period. At the same time, we can find within material life that archetypal purity—that's one of the differences among different schools. Some want to *escape* from physical life, and just want to go to the transcendent. Others say: "As above, so below. *It's right here!* I find it *right here*; right here at this time—not at some future date."

When we look at Genesis we see several key areas for discussion: creation of the cosmos, creation of man and woman, the naming of the animals, and the fall from grace and original sin.

The creation of the cosmos is out of *nothingness*, or the "negative" Limitless Light of Kabbalah. This is the *Ain*, the *Ain Soph*, the *Ain Soph Aur*—the negative, limitless light. This is a great void. I like Isaac Luria because he spends a great deal of time talking about the Ain Soph. One of the errors we make in modern Kabbalah is that we talk almost exclusively about Kether. You're still dealing, at that point, with what we call "First Cause" (or, in Gnostic terms, the Demiurge). What we really want to look at is the Void.

[Audience Member: Does that involve the "Qabalistic Cross" when you're connecting to Kether?]

Yes, you are connecting to Kether, but Kether is really connecting to the Void. If you look closely at the way a lot of the teachings are given, you're *not* connecting with the Void, you're connecting with something "right on the edge" of it. So you have to open it up more; you have to push the boundary of it more, and that will suffice.

It's because it's a *notion*, it's all just a notion. If you really *could* connect with it, then—wow! Please take a seat!

I mean that seriously. We talk about these things in ways as if they're incredibly concrete, as if it's very simple. It's not—it's a progressive process, and that progressive process is all within us.

Man is an expression of this All—Adam, the First Man. An expression of this all-encompassing power. It was created in part by the Secondary Causes, or the Elohim. This is where we hear: "Let *us* create man in our own image." The Elohim or Secondary Causes are *forces of nature*. So we could say that the forces of nature bring things into being. Maybe consciousness wasn't such an idea, in the sense that, "Hey, we're going to make this." These forces, just through their inner actions, give rise to something.

This is one of the possibilities of it. The other is that we have within us all of these other forces which we would call the "planetary" forces, the "Elemental" forces, etc. These in part can be represented by the [30:18, pt. 2].

It's interesting because this power is expressed in two forms. In one of the Creation stories (there are two of them in Genesis), Adam is originally bisexual in nature, because woman (Eve) is taken out of him. When we talk about "Eve" esoterically, we're talking about *expressed Creation*, duality in the world of form that we can identify with. Form-giving things.

In another part, Eve is created and then *presented* to Adam. Regardless of this, it is a Golden Age, an archetypal world that we're talking about—not something literal.

In the Garden of Eden there are many trees, some say ten. In the middle of them are the Tree of Life and the Tree of the Knowledge of Good and Evil. Our work is often with the Tree of Life, particularly Luria's Tree of Life. Upon eating of the Tree of the Knowledge of Good and Evil, they saw that they were naked, and they were ashamed and hid from God. This simply means that in Eden, their original state, they are in a primordial bliss. There's no sense of duality, there's no sense of "otherness." Whatever thoughts arose of attraction and repulsion—which are just the forces in our being, fight or flight, attraction and repulsion, "want" and "don't want," these are primal motivators—created shame, meaning a feeling of ego or inadequacy.

This is the beginning of neurotic thought. Dubuis would say that in the primordial state, the Fall was a willful thing, which is another story that works as well. Out of primordial bliss was this ignorance, and in order to *know*, to become *self-aware*, we have to have *separation*, or that sense of separation.

In Western esotericism, in Kabbalah and magic, we look at

the Fall in two ways. One, again, as this *error*, in which we're trying to re-integrate into this primordial archetypal unity. This we call it the "Path of Return"; we call the fruits of the Path of Return *re-integration*, re-integration into the whole. Also, we look at it as a *willful decision*, like the prodigal son who leaves and then comes back, because then he will have something to offer.

We come down, we come in ignorance. You see this notion of the Fall and the Return—involution and evolution—at different schools constantly taking place. This is nice because that means our "wretched state" is not only temporary, but is also something that we can get a purpose from: *to become self-aware.* Again, going back to Éliphas Lévi's statement, the purpose of the Great Work is for each person to fully express and manifest the powers within and of themselves.

What are those powers? The powers which we call the Kingdom of Heaven; the archetypal purity which exists *within us.* We have to pull that out, we have to uncover that.

The archetypal bliss has no room for duality. That's why we talked about *focusing on this joy* earlier when you were doing the meditation. Focusing on this happiness—because with that there's no room for duality, there's no room for separation. Although in the beginning it's going to be artificial for you, it's going to be contrived, and you may think, "Oh, I'm *faking* it"—well, that's all right. That's all we do in life. Whether you "fake it 'til you make it," as they say in recovery circles, or whether you keep doing Assumption of the Godform until it might *work.* You just keep habituating yourself to the ideas and the notions that you want, and the feelings that go with them, and they will grow over time.

We need to be careful here because it's easy to slip into a kind of dualism here where the material world is meant to be "shunned." We see that in some teachings—but it's *not.* It's part of the practice. Particularly in this, the "Age of Iron," the Age of the Wolf, the Kali Yuga, the material world is our jumping-off pad, it's part of the process.

In the eighteenth century school the Elus Cohens of Pasqualez, the Fall of Man was seen as similar to the murder of Osiris, in which Adam fell to pieces, and these pieces each contained a divine spark; they make up all the members of humanity, and it is humanity's task to re-integrate them into the whole. That's interesting because one of the divine sparks that fall *before* that creates the Qliphoth, or the "Shells." These become what we call the "demonic forces."

These negative forces slither upon the Earth; they are represented by the serpent in the Garden of Eden. They are not to be abandoned, however, but rather *pulled forth with us*, as our earlier prayers mentioned, because they contain a spark of the divine as well. It is in their salvation, within us—again, these would be our neurotic tendencies, our own self-limiting notions, our own negative feelings toward ourself and others—when overcome, we accomplish our Work, our assistance to others, and at the same time have a *fact* that reaches beyond our mere mind into the actual material world itself. At that point, the notion of *separation* has been radically thinned.

By integrating and overcoming our own neurotic tendencies—which we see as the demonic forces—by pulling them within us and integrating them, we recognize that divine spark that is *everywhere*, doing that *repair* of the early work.

[Audience Member: So, it's accepting your "dark side."]

Right. Transforming it with Light, and realizing that their *is* no "light" and "dark" side. Within Lurianic Kabbalah—very similar to the writings of Jacob Boehme—there is the blissful, loving God, and there's the severe God. But they're *both* God. What do they do? What we've done is that we tend to think of spirituality as "always being nice," and it is true that we have to be kind to one another and generous, and I do not wish to offend you, or anyone here. But sometimes, when people ask questions, if they really want the answer, you have to be careful. Do you really want the answer, that is, something that will help you? Or do you simply want me to reinforce your own neurotic thinking? Because *that's* not helping you! So there's going to be an abrasive period where: "I don't *like* that! I don't *like* you! You said something *bad* to me! You're supposed to approve of me and love me as I *am*! Don't be so *judgmental*—that's not *spiritual*!"

Hey! *Get over it!* [laughter] How you treat others is important—but treating others means "do unto others as you would have others do unto you." So I don't want people to simply *lie* to me. What if the king has no clothes? If I'm walking around in my underwear, *tell me!* (Thanks, I appreciate it!) [laughter] I left the marble boxers at home! [laughter]

[Audience Member: What is this neurotic force?]

I think a lot of it has to do with the separation of the material and physical is very difficult on this level. There is a lot of overlap, so the conditioning takes place often in the nervous system. Those of you who do body therapies and yoga know that these emotions somatize in the body. That's why we say: "Forgive me, for I have sinned in thought, word, and deed." I have made mistakes in my *thoughts*, in my *speech*, and in my *actions*.

So *don't* sin in thought, word, and deed! Our thoughts, our words, and our actions become the tools for integration, as expressed in ritual work. We do certain things, we say certain prayers, we think certain ideas, and it all begins in the mind. The mind has ideas and when they hold on to them powerfully they become *emotionalized*, and those emotions then create tensions in the body. Those tensions in the body, it's believed—now, this is purely esoteric, please understand— actually make a mark or imprint in the psychic body. Images are actually held there. I think this is true to some degree.

This is then transmitted on from generation to generation; recall talking about the "seventh generation." We change our physical structure—this is getting somewhat beyond the scope, now—as a result of these practices. It has an effect on them. To think that's limited to *me* is not true—it's passed on to my children. So it acts as an *opportunity* for them—it doesn't necessarily guarantee anything.

[Audience Member: Do they serve a purpose, though?]

Everything we do has a purpose. We talked about that last time, with values. Values are what we get rewarded for. That's why we form them—we get rewarded for them. So what was valuable in one setting may not be valuable in another, but if we're habituated—unconsciously doing the same thing—then we run into problems.

[Audience Member: Expecting it to be valued.]

But it's not. Now, this is an *easy* example—there are many that are more subtle, and I'll try to think of them. But consider post-traumatic stress disorder. You see these veterans who are exposed to *powerful* emotional situations, and powerful emotional situations are the cause of the psychic knot. That's it. That's what causes the imprint on the mind and on the body. So they are exposed to this, and then they're rewarded for certain behaviors when that takes place. But there's external stimuli that bring it into motion—external stimuli or sounds, *phonemes*, that cause an emotional trigger. There's external visual things that cause it.

I forget the name of the author, but he was a British soldier during the First World War, and he wrote a book called *Goodbye to All That*. In it, he talked about going home on leave from Belgium in 1915 or 1916 or whatever it was, and he said that he couldn't relax, he couldn't enjoy leave, because as he was walking through the countryside he would be thinking: "Oh, that would be a nice place for a machine gun..." That's what has been imprinted on him, and he *knows* this, he recognizes this, and that's why you end up with the "Lost Generation."

[Audience Member: Those behaviors were validated in situations of survival.]

That's exactly right, it was *survival*. We don't exist in a survival situation anymore, so we really don't understand the way a large part of the world *was*, and still *is*. That's very important. What you need to do under *one* situation is not necessarily what you need to do in another, and what we're looking at is trying to find some kind of *mechanism* where we can not simply be acting habituated to situations but, instead, begin to perceive a larger picture of *truth*, that allows us to say, "Well, this is the *right* action for this situation, and this is the right action that will allow either the most benefit for everyone or the least harm." Rather than just "stimuli-response, stimuli-response, stimuli-response." That's where the original fall is, described one way: it's simply a stimulus-response mechanism.

Now, stimulus-response allows us to think: "There might be *more* to this!" [laughter] Wake up—fall asleep; wake up— fall asleep; wake up—fall asleep... But it's *still* stimulus- response. You really only dedicate yourself truly to spiritual practices when you think there's a *payoff*. The payoff was: "I wanna work *magic* so I can *get stuff!* 'Cause my life *sucks* and I don't really wanna *change* things!" [laughter]

Stimulus-response. That's kind of working well...but not as well as I thought! So how about... And it goes from there. It goes from very narrow to very wide. Originally, it was very wide to very narrow; now, it's very narrow to very wide. Or "broader," if you will.

So now we also have the Psalms. The Psalms, or the Songs of David, are the most commonly used part of the Old Testament for esoteric work. The one you heard at the beginning was the Ninety-first Psalm, and that, of course, is always said prior to magical operations. You can learn them, sing them in Latin if you like, do it in Hebrew. I don't really care. Do them in whatever language you like. The Psalms also have Divine Names that are associated with them; you can find that in the fourth appendix of the *Sixth & Seventh Books of Moses.*

You have the Gospel of John. This is the most esoteric of all the gospels. It is not a synoptic gospel, meaning that if you take Matthew, Mark, and Luke, and you line them up—even though Mark is the smallest gospel, and, I believe,

Matthew is the longest—you see roughly a similar pattern of story developing. The Gospel of John is different. This is where we have, "In the beginning was the Word," or, as we say, "In principio ad Verbum." There's much discussion about what that "Word" actually might have meant.

You find that the Gospel of John is often used during various initiations that use a Bible, which will be open to that gospel. Some organizations will do their openings using "In the Name of" meaning "In the Power" or "In the Creative Essence." That's what we mean by "Name." We say, "In the Name of the Father, and of the Son, and of the Holy Spirit," or "In the Name of the Holy Trinity," or some groups will do it "In the Name of St. John."

"John" is more esoteric. There are also some references in it that had occurred prior to the destruction of Jerusalem, so earlier readers didn't know. They weren't sure about it, and they hung out on the fringes for a long time.

Then there's the Book of Revelation. This is the most difficult book of the New Testament, in that it is completely symbolic and has several levels of meaning. These levels include a *historical* meaning, relevant to the early period of Christianity. Many people say that the Book of Revelation deals with the early Christian experience. You have a second interpretation which says that this is a *prophecy* of events to occur in the future at the end of the Christian era, but, within that context, it also means "history as we know it." Again, this is because the idea is one of linear motion, rather than a cyclical one.

Esoterically, it's cyclical—it's just the end of the era and, of course, in the Gospel it talks about the end of the *age*, not the "end of the world." The end of the *age*; the end of the *era*.

Jean Dubuis had stated that it was a text of Christian initiation of an interior level, which we'll talk about, and a sort of "guidebook" for the souls of the dead within the Christian context (which I think is partially true). Any effort to attempt to interpret the Book of Revelation in a singular way *will be false.*

Now, it's very important to understand that *your* understanding of the Revelation of St. John is formed by a uniquely (not only) Western church perspective, but Western *Protestant* perspective. Even Kelpius thought that the Second Coming was at hand. If you had survived the Thirty Years' War, or had been descendents of those who had survived it, then you probably would, too. Again, those experiences shaped and formed philosophy and the spirituality of the people. The closest example I can give you is this: it took *two hundred years* for central Europe, including Germany, to get *back* the same level of infrastructure it had in 1615. Two hundred years!

Think of this: you have massive movements of people across the countryside. You have foreign armies traipsing across the place for thirty years, off and on. You have no gold. You have no silver. You're down to what's called the "copper standard." So, if you have some copper, that's the only precious metal valued, outside of steel. That's the level of suffering that all of central Europe experienced for almost two generations, thirty years. It had a profound effect on what they thought was happening.

This was so horrible that *of course* "Jesus had to be coming back"! This is what was described! How could it be worse than *this*? It couldn't, honestly.

It didn't happen, and those views fall. Come and go; come and go. But the notion or the hope of it was embedded in them, and Jacob Boehme always talked about the "Time of the Lily," that future time when everything would be made right. Everything would be brought back to primordial harmony. They kept hoping for it.

Within the Eastern Orthodox Tradition—and this is important to note—the Revelation of John is viewed as a book that is never read during the liturgy. It's viewed as a liturgical text. So, this Revelation of John is not a historical event;

their interpretation is very mystical, very esoteric. It is not a historical event that will take place at some time in the future or that has taken place at some time in the past—it is *currently happening*, right now—again, going back to Dubuis's idea that it's an initiatic text. That's why we see in French esotericism a lot of the moderns are quasi-Orthodox in their orientation, even if they're Roman Catholic.

That is really the way it needs to be read: as an *unfolding pattern*, right now. Let us look at the words so that we know they're right: Jesus Christ is the source of salvation. Jesus Christ is who? That is the descent of the godhead into matter that comes to redeem humanity; that is the spiritual force fully present, uncorrupted—meaning, with no neurotic tendencies, if you want to call it that. No scoria; nothing was corrupted in the Fall, as you see in the Gnostic texts where Sophia is mangled and raped along the way until she's barely recognizable in the end, and then works her way back up. No—this is a descent, fully complete. The Light is expressed fully and completely to all beings. It brings Light, therefore the Illumination continues to grow and spread. With that light we overcome our notions of "I" and "Thou." As with the Lord's Prayer: there's no "I" in it. You're praying for *everyone* when you pray it.

With that, you get salvation, which is the return to unity, to that primordial awareness. I don't like the word "unity," but that's the one we find most often used. It is a primordial or pure awareness, where those mental errors no longer exist—we've cleansed those.

Now, of course, we say that Jesus Christ can be looked at as a historical person, which is essential for much of the magic, but, at the same time, as a *force*, an archetypal force, and, again and again, one we receive reference to: Christ *within*. That's very important because in the magic that we'll talk about this afternoon, it's always about "these things which I have done, so shall you do," which you see in the Gospel. People call on the Name of Jesus Christ within the context of the Bible; they call on John within the context of the Bible; they call on the Father, Son, and Holy Ghost within the context of the Scriptures. For example, "as Moses has done this" or "as Solomon has done this" or "as David has done this, so do I do." That is, in its own way, an Assumption of the Godform.

They have done it; they have done it through this power, I can do it as well. This is *very* important. This *has* been done, this is *being* done, and this *will be done* in the future. This *has* been done, this is *being* done, and this *will be* done. This was not a one-time event, and all this is within me, too. So all of these self-limiting feelings, all of these feelings of inadequacy, all of these pity parties that go on—these are not present.

This way, God is the source of all; the Son is our inner, direct nature of perception; and the Holy Spirit or Shekhinah is the creative, life energies that permeate the visible and invisible realms. Remember, though, it's in *duality*—we are in the presence of the Deity, right here, right now.

Again, the Father is the source of all being, it is *everything*, all. The Son is our direct perception of actuality. We use two terms: reality and actuality. You've heard the terms "relative" and "absolute." Relative is from *my* perception; absolute is what *is*. I was brought up with the terms *reality* and *actuality*. Actuality is what *is*; reality is *relative* to one's perception. That would be duality versus the picture, the joke being that, well, first of all, there's no such thing as an "automobile accident" in a police report. There's "automobile collisions." So those of you who understand the difference, get it! [laughter] The reason being is that whenever you have a *collision* you have two parties and some witnesses, and whatever number of people that adds up to, that's how many different stories you have. That would be "reality."

Now, one of those people standing on the street corner might actually have seen the whole thing, and they can tell you what *actually* happened. So, *actuality* is what's actually going on, uncorrupted, unobscured—and that's the Son. That's the Christ; that's direct perception, because on the Tree of Life we give that to Tiphareth, and that is united to all the spheres. That's the heart, the heart-mind. That's we have to open the heart-mind and expand it.

The Holy Spirit, then, is often called the female presence or feminine presence of deity; the immanent presence of God. That's the initiatic power, if you want to know. That's why you'll see, in most of the initiations in the classical world, women are given as the initiatic force—pleasantly dressed in red if dressed at all.

♱ ❀ ♰

◇ PART THREE ◇

What we're going to talk about this afternoon is cleansing of obstacles, some healing practices, and what we generally look at under the heading of exorcism, although not in the sense that you may think of it as "demonic" exorcism. We're looking at this as *cleansing*, or getting rid of things—"cleaning the plate," if you will.

The important part here is that suffering is part of the human condition. If you look at the magical operations listed in all the books, very rarely are they about some kind of "divine awakening." Usually, it's "heal my dog," "heal my cow," "heal my broken leg," "heal my sick baby—let's not die in childbirth." It's stuff that we don't think about nowadays. So the nature of the human condition required that magic be something that would, essentially, keep us alive. Once that was taken care of, it might be other things: how to be protected from robbers, how to be victorious in battle, how to have a safe journey—you'd be surprised how many prayers and charms there are just for a safe journey. We don't think about that.

We complain about having to take our shoes off and instrusive X-rays! But in reality traveling was very dangerous. A lot of it had to do with things like the weather—what we traveled through up here. The famous "Donner Pass" party— "Oh! We'll stop here—and then eat each other for the next three months!" [laughter] We don't think about that kind of thing because we fundamentally have *easy travel*, which is a good thing. I like it!

However, we have to recognize that the magical practices we're looking at really come from a different time. So, what we need to do is basically clear obstacles from our Path of Return. By doing practical things—by clearing obstacles out of our daily path, whether it be health or illness or problematic neighbors or poor conditions of whatever sort—the theory is (and the idea behind it should be) that I'm doing this so that I can continue my Work, my unfoldment, my awakening. Why? So that I can be helpful to others, to every being that there is.

Remember the early prayer we did: *all* these beings, visible, invisible, human, not human, what-have-you. That's our motivation, and as we set that up as our motivation, of course, it has a broader reach, a broader impact, in Nature because more beings are assisted by it, and Nature will put more of itself behind it.

I like this from the old Greek text *On the Mysteries*: "We should not be afraid to say this thing as well, and that is we frequently need to perform rituals on account of pressing bodily needs, for the gods and the good demons of the body." The good spirits, the good gods. We're doing these rituals just to get through the day.

Fortunately, we have some luxury in our life and we don't have to be that pressed; we are allowed to expand that to a little more idealistic notion. We still, though, need to make offerings—and offerings are one of those things that are *so rarely done* today. You see them in a lot of shamanic practices, you see them in a lot of Oriental practices, but the notion of an offering in Western esotericism is only loosely survived in the notion of the Eucharist. That's one of the few places where it survives, where we see ritual sacrifice and redemption.

That's really just a religious thing; but, again, in ancient times there was really no separation between these magical and mystical and religious activities. They were all flowing into one another.

Agrippa talks a great deal in the *Fourth Book*, and also in the *Third Book*, about offerings. An offering is a form of sacrifice. The reason we make offerings—and even Isaac Luria talks about offerings and the role of sacrifice in redemption—is to overcome our selfishness, to overcome our stinginess and our self-centeredness. That's the reason we make them.

Some people also view it as a kind of payment, and on a magical level, it sort of is, although not completely. It can be a kind of payment sometimes to various entities or beings that my be involved in the activity we're engaged in. In that case, the payment is often one of an etheric nature, meaning the things which are offered are *scents*. You'll notice that *scent* is very strong.

Notice that we're talking about the Element of Air. Air is that *pneuma*, that vital force and energy that pervades all things, pervades us, pervades our blood. They say that before a being is re-incarnated, what attracts it most is *smell*. We don't really think in those terms that much these days, but that's important to know. It's the *smell*. These odors—pleasant odors or non-pleasant odors—are all vaporous energy that the invisible world is attracted to. That's why we burn incense: to create a pleasant condition for spiritual vibration. Not just "vibration"—who cares about "vibration"? But for *intelligence*—for *intelligences* or *beings* or *forces* to come into our world.

The reason for this is very simple: we *smell* to them. In fact, it is stated in some places that the angels find our smell *repulsive*.

[Audience Member: Even after we shower?]

Even after we shower, yeah! Now, whether that is true or not, it's the point that ritual cleanliness is important. Ritual cleanliness can, of course, become dogmatic and be taken too far—"I just can't *do* anything! I haven't *properly prepared!*" No—you have to prepare, but ritual cleanliness is not just of the body, but of the *mind*.

Remember: *thought, word,* and *deed*. It's of our *speech*, it's of our *emotions*—all of these levels. In this cleanliness we develop around us what is called the "odor of sanctity." That odor of sanctity is often reported to smell very specifically like *roses*. That's why sometimes, in your periods of practice, you may smell *perfume*, particularly a kind of "rosy" scent, spontaneously. Has anyone experienced that? It's the odor of sanctity. From some people, it emanates from them all the time, through their psychic channels, their psychic body, because there's nothing to block the free flow of this energy, which permeates it.

You have to create the proper causes and conditions for the being to manifest. We use incense of different types to attract different types of spirits or beings, or even just an ethereal, abstract, archetypal vibration, if you will, because smell is the oldest part of our brain and, of course, is the most linked to memory. The oldest part of our brain is the strongest when it comes to what we think of as "psychic" or "paranormal" phenomena.

So odor is extremely important in this work, but with that is the actually act of breathing itself, physical breathing. One of the ways we cleanse is by the breath; one of the ways we breath is by the breath. Breath is linked to our emotional states; you know that when you breathe quickly and heavily from the top, you're very excited. When you breathe slowly, you're more centered. When you breathe deeply, you feel not only centered but *relaxed, euphoric, expanded*—you also feel *warmth* or *heat*.

Here we have the Elements: Fire, Air, Water, Earth. It is the Air that allows us to access that Cosmic Fire. We don't touch the Fire directly, we *breathe it in* through the Air, and from there it goes into our bloodstream. That's our Water—it circulates throughout our whole body. From there, it sinks into the bones, into the flesh, into the muscles—and that's Earth. This cycle then continues.

This psychic energy, this *pneuma*, this breath is always constantly circulating. It circulates across the world according to astrological cycles; it circulates in us according to our breathing in cycles as well.

When we talk about offerings, we're talking about offerings

in *generosity*, of the heart. These offerings can be to specific spirits—I've seen that done. It can be in general. It can be offerings of thanksgiving, rather than offerings used to energize a ritual, which I'm not very fond of. I think they should be just offerings of thanksgiving and generosity.

We also see these offerings in some ways in the ancient Egyptian temples, when they would put fruit and all these things next to the temple, or inside of the tomb. They did this to appease the spirits, to feed the mummy.

They specifically say that the spirits didn't sustain themselves off the fruit—but, rather, off the *essence* of the fruit, the *odor*. The smell. Smells are very powerful in attracting the dead as well.

One of the ways of making offerings later on—because people didn't have a lot of money—was to make offerings of food or flowers, and this is very good. I remember one woman whom I met earlier this year who was telling me how her lama had said to her that it's really not a good idea to make flower offerings at a cemetery because the spirits of the dead smell those, they're attracted to them, and they may follow you home. I thought that was very interesting. I don't necessarily agree with it in that regard, but I do understand the theory behind it.

We use these odors and these senses to create a link with the invisible world; we use these physical things, through their essence, to create a link with the invisible world. At some point, we look at offerings as a way of paying off our *debt*. How can I, if you will, lighten my "karmic load"? My "baggage of sin" or error? How can I lighten that up?

This process of offerings became abused during the Middle Ages in terms of making donations to the Church. It's very important that we support and make donations to spiritual practices, to spiritual processes, because that is the only thing that is going to really get us out of this confused state of suffering. It's very important that we do that on different levels. But here what had happened is it became a way of, basically, people trying to "buy" their way out of Hell, or buy their way out of something.

You can understand how that could easily become popular; but you can't necessarily buy your way out of things. It just doesn't work that way; it's not a *quid pro quo*. You *can* recognize that you've made an error in your life. You can recognize specifically what that error was. You can resolve to *never do it again*, and you can make efforts of *sacrifice*, of *petition* if you will, to make things "better" in some fashion.

This is a notion, of course, that we generally don't think of in Western magic, because we're just going to "move stuff around"—"get them spirits to do what we want!" Well, not necessarily—they know you better than you know yourself. They can see what your deepest motivation is (or at least your motivation at the moment) because it is just an energy field to them, it's a vibration, it's an emotion. You know how we pick up on the emotions of others? Just think how much easier it is for *them* without the blocks in the way.

So I encourage you to undertake the practice of making offerings regularly. The best day of the week is either a Thursday or a Friday—Friday is wonderful. I have a prayer that's attached for these general offerings, and you'll notice that the prayers come from the *Hymns of Orpheus*.[1] You can use anything you want on the plate. I came across a fairly nice silver plate in a Salvation Army somewhere, and right on top of it was a dessert bowl. It's nice that it was silver, and the dessert bowl is a glass insert, so I can take the glass insert and fill it up with whatever I want.

What do we fill it up with? Those things which are attractive, those things which are valuable, those things which are pretty. Those things which *you would like to receive yourself.* Remember: we're looking to find a way to make ourselves—I don't like the word "attractive," but maybe that's it—of *value* to others. "This guy or this woman isn't just calling

---

[1]See pages 68-70 and Appendix of present text.

me to do something for them, and then there's just going to tell me to get out." That's just looking at it from the level of spirit interaction, which is really a fairly low activity, by the way. Really it is, and it rarely works out in your favor, because people do it when they're desperate, and then the entity or being *knows* you're desperate and jerks you around! [laughter]

Everyone I know who has done this tells the same story! "Oh, the more I made offerings, the less I got!" Yeah, because— first of all—you're stupid! [laughter] You were desperate, they knew you were desperate, *I* can see the desperation all over you—what do you think *they* could see? They can *smell* it, literally—the stink of adrenaline coming off of you. "Oh, I've *gotta* get this to *work*!"

That's the last minute stuff, rather than how do I become a *decent human being*, you see? When we make these general offerings, it's about *how do we help others*, not what do we get in return. All your donations, all your offerings should be like that.

We were talking last night about *service*, and how to be of service. The best way is anonymously. As a Freemason, I take great pride in telling people that the Freemasons donate about a million to two million dollars a day to charitable practices. How do they do it? Quietly. Masonry says: "We make good men better." You don't do that by taking credit for everything you do that's good. They have twenty-three children's burn hospitals operated *free of charge* across the country. *All* free of charge. I'll pick you up and drop you off, too, if you don't have a vehicle. You don't see it in the paper; you don't see them broadcasting it. Because that's just what you do. Rotary is another one.

I tell people it's great if you're going to buy "organically grown, fair-trade coffee" and eat all the right stuff and make sure that there aren't too many animal products in your shoes, but at the same time, wear all hemp, so there's no suspicious chemicals either, so we can be in tune with nature...that's wonderful. But did you help fix the playground down the street? If you don't help your neighbor—if you don't even know who they *are*—then your donations are just, well, they're *helpful*, but they're not what they *fully* could be.

As we hear in the ancient texts: "Each according to their ability and each according to their need." Each man performs his service to the holy in accordance of what he *is*, not according to what he is *not*. After all, sacrifice must not surpass the proper measure of the worshipper.

We're dealing with what we *can* be, what we are *not* as a limited neurotic being—what are we *fully*? What is our *fullest potential*? That involves the people around you. What are you doing locally? Rotary is great. You see it in the paper once in a while, but you hardly ever hear about most of what they do. I find it interesting that, of all the organizations that are quickly and immediately suppressed during a Nazi or Communist regimes, the two that stood out most were Freemasonry and Rotary. Why? Because of those things I just mentioned.

That's the *true* generation and expression of generosity: helping others, helping your community, and being useful. You have to do that *as well as* making these offerings. Prayers alone are *not enough*. They're *good* and they're *helpful*, and they're the *starting point*—but they're *not* the end-point.

As they say, "Praise the Lord and pass the ammunition!" [laughter]

An offering plate can be anything. You can have some incense on it, some nice crystals, nice jewels and shiny things, some food products, some sweets, some sours, some food. Anything that anyone might like. Have some wine and water with it, as an offering on the side. We then say the Orphic Hymn:

> Hearken, Divinities!
> You who hold the reigns of sacred wisdom,

Who set men's souls on fire with flames invulnerable,
Drawing them through the cloudy depths
Far up to the immortals;
Purging us with mystic rites
Of indescribable hymns.
Hearken, Great Saviors!
From divine books, grant me the innocent,
Blameless light that dissipates the clouds,
So that I may discover the Truth,
That man is immortal divinity.
Either the evil-working spirits restrain me,
Under the Lethean waters of oblivion,
Ever far from the blessed,
From my soul would no longer continue to stray,
Nor suffer the cruel pains of imprisonment in the
    bonds of life,
May gods of high and illustrious wisdom,
Masters and leaders—hear me!
And hasten along the upward way!
Initiate me into the *orgiac* mysteries,
And reveal them, by the ceremonies of sacred words!

Imagine at this time that all those people you have said prayers for are now with you. All those beings. Here, you have *everything*, like a giant Santa Claus or cornucopia, to give to them whatever they wish.

Sophia, all-encircling goddess, whose embrace with the All-Father gives rise to pure desire, and birth to all the worlds and their children. Your tender kiss renews all life and stirs our sleeping mind to awakening. Move us from ignorance and suffering to wisdom and bliss! Accept this, our fleshy offering, and bless it so that all the demons and guardians who dwell here joyfully receive it, and their happiness clears away all obstacles from our path, and that they defend us on our way. Bless this we drink, that the ghosts who wander through our domain are satisfied, their hunger and thirst quenched, turning their sorrows into joy so that they may be guided and guide others, upward on the Path of Return. Bless this our perfume, that those who wander in the heavenly realms, ascending and descending into the earthly realms, may hear our prayers and be justly guided into the kingdom of light, and hailed as returning heroes, conquerors of the indomitable citadel. Bless this sacred wine, nectar of the gods, with the full power of life. Mercury, the eternal, young, and immortal one, lord of the two lands, is eternally awakened within us. And let the demigods and angels pour forth their holy power into our work, and in turn be blessed with eternal life. Bless this offering stone that it may bear witness to our sincerity and devotion to the work, that the power of the gods is born, raised, and eternally lives within me, as that within which we live, move, and have our being. May all the archangels and gods know life and light eternal, and fear death no more. Bless these offered jewels, and all the beings be blessed with wealth, health, capacity of mind, pure desire, and leisure to undertake the Lightning Path of Return to the Eternal. Hear these, our prayers, your children, your sons and daughters. Amen.

Then just place it outside for a night. Put it out, and the animals come and eat it, whatever.

As you can see, there's a lot of good things that are mentioned, representing all the things that are desirable and good. I pulled that particular Hymn of Orpheus from my great-uncle's notebooks. This is important, because this is the foundation of our work—it is our beginning. The broader our beginning, the broader our possible results. It's that simple. The narrower our beginning, the narrower our results. That's it.

It also helps to cleanse away fear, because you are afraid of these beings, inherently. You fear them. Those of you whose knees start knocking together when we mention the demons and ghosts—"What do you *mean*, I'm going to invite them here?!?" Well, because right now they are a problem to you, and you've got to talk to them because they are a problem to you, and find out how you can get them *not* to be a problem for you! This is one of the ways.

The gods and demigods don't really *care* about you. You're a minor annoyance to them at best. So how are you going to *get* them to care about you? You show them that you're someone worth caring about.

Fortunately, the enlightened beings and the saints, the avatars, whatever you want to call them, they *do* care about you! That's they're only saving grace! But most of the universe is like *you*! They don't *care*! [laughter] So you've got to change that.

[Audience Member: So are you saying that the offerings we're doing in this practice are not just important for *us*, but also for *everything?*]

Yes, because you're not limiting here. Everything! Everyone. Even the animals eat it, they're hungry.

[Audience Member: Raccoons.]

Let the raccoons eat it—they'll enjoy it. Especially the M & Ms, right?

Now, that's the offering; that's generosity, that's important. Again, the best time to do that is a Friday, but Thursdays are good as well.

So, you've done that—that's nice, but now I've got some stuff I've got to do. I've got to get *rid* of some things. I need to make what we call an *extraction*, if you will. There's something *bothering* me; there's an illness going on. There is a disturbance in the Force!

It's a funny thing to see—I can theorize why it works, I can't tell you why. I have an idea. When you look at German magic—folk magic of any kind—you're looking at several areas. One is the notion of *contagion*. One is *similarity*, and the other is contagion. "Similarity" means "like is like"; we call that correspondences. "Contagion" means *contagious*—it can *move*. So psychic energies are *contagious*; that's why stale breath, stale airs, places where the air doesn't move—that's why in *feng shui* this is *bad news*. The *life force* is out of it; the life force is depleted. When you are in a place where the life force is depleted, what does it do?

Just like a battery: you put your batteries together, you make a daisy chain of batteries, and what's going to happen? If you have some that are drained down, the rest go down to that level, too.

So that's what happens. Very simple. This isn't rocket science. You always want to make sure that you're always in an environment where the energy level is high. You do that with nice colors, nice and bright; lots of green plants, living plants, preferably, but even just green-colored ones are good. Some nice odors.

I *still* can remember the *stench* of Slocum Hall on Sunday morning at nine a.m., 1982! [laughter] It was *always there*. It didn't move—always that foul stench.

My kids wanted to go bowling, so we went to this one bowling alley, and even though they hadn't been smoking in them for *years*, it still has that *wonderful* stench of stale cigarettes and spilled beer. I said, "No, kids, we're not going to go anywhere near there...!" [laughter] Just because of the smell; and what does a smell do to *you*? It changes your emotions, very quickly.

Immediately, it can be a negative emotional state, which is a negative *physical* state, and therefore a negative mental state. If you can learn to be imperturbable—indifferent—you'll learn to move through. Don't worry about it; comes and goes. But many people aren't there. That's something they're working towards.

So, if we are not able to deal with that, not able to transform that negative state, what we do is avoid it and create positive ones. At this stage of the game we're dealing *not* with transformation, but with "getting rid of" and positive states. That needs to be very clear. We'll deal with transformation later on.

These are stages, and they're not clear-cut, by the way. I just tell them to you as if they are. Each one of us is different.

One of the wonderful things to do in order to extract something is, if you have a disease, if you or someone has something wrong with them—and I know you've all done this, because Brian and I talked about it—then it needs a place to *go*. Remember, in the Gospel of Mark, what's the first thing he does? He casts the demons out of the sick man, and they say, "We are Legion. We are many. Oh, do not send us there! Do not send us to the abyss—give us a place!" And he sends them into the swine.

They want a home, because in that ethereal state it's chaos. That's why you reincarnate: because you can't handle being out of your body. This is *safe* for you. That's why when people are astral projecting they think, "Oh, man! It feels like I'm going to die!" They pop back into their bodies—now it's back into "safety zone." This is a barrier between you and the other world.

That's why we practice Assumption of the Godform, so that we can create this form for ourselves, this expression, so that when we are no longer physically involved—whether in death or in out-of-body experiences or in sleep when we dream—we have an image to project; a body, if you will, a sense of boundary, if you will, when we're in this sea of energetic environments.

Also, importantly, *as you see yourself, so do the invisible see you.* So if you see yourself as Tahuti or one of the gods, that's how they see you. If you see yourself as a quivering, begging mass, they see you as *lunch*! [laughter] Okay? That's very important to know!

How you see yourself in this life, in this world, and in the other, is what is projected out. It all folds back onto itself. So the more confident you are, the more comfortable you are, the more *courageous* you are, the easier you will go through *this* life and the easier you will go through the other worlds. When we deal with actual demons, the only thing they really have to offer is *fear—your* fear.

You must have the knowledge that there is power and strength in yourself, that there's nothing to be afraid of. I'll talk about some examples of that later.

"Contagious" works with a living thing, and though it's improper for us to baptize a frog and name it, to send some evil to it—as we often hear—something to which you *can* do this is an *egg*, because an egg is not fertilized, therefore it's not technically alive, if you will. It is, however, an organic, physical, material container.

It's a growth medium. You take the egg and you rub it over the person with the idea that you are extracting out or pulling out whatever it is that's bothering them. Pulling it out, into the egg.

What I'm telling you now is very general, because when we move on to other practices I'm going to talk about facing "this" direction and facing "that" direction and these types of things, but not now. Right now we're just going to talk about general things.

You take the egg afterward and you wrap it in black and red yarn or string.

When you go back and look at the symbolism of the egg, at the same time, let me tell you that one of the more unique symbols of the egg is that you see one of the stories goes—and, of course, these are teaching stories, not meant to be taken literally, although many people do take them that way—that Mary Magdalene presented a red egg to Caesar. I thought that was fascinating—the red egg, because the egg is not only so symbolic of life, but also here is the Philosopher's Stone, and it's Mary Magdalene who presents it. Remember: it's *always* going to be the "woman in red" who is the initiatic force, literally and figuratively. (Except for some ladies, for whom it might be a little different.) However, most of the time, when we see it, it's going to be that way.

You rub the egg over the person in a straight motion, usually from the *center*, out. Moving away and down; top-down, center-out. The idea is that you are *collecting* this. It's all being pulled into the egg. Honestly, everyone I know who has done this has had a different prayer. There's no standardized prayer for it. I knew one person who did the "wart-removing prayer," which is generally done according to the cycles of the moon. They did a variation of that: "That which I see, decrease; that which I rub, decrease." And the reverse if you want something to grow: "That which I see, increase; that which I rub, increase." The former removes the warts.

They would do the same thing with the egg, a variation on that. The whole notion, though, is that for your purpose, your focus, whatever prayer or chant that you want to make up for it needs to be easily repeatable. You're pulling it all in. The words themselves put you in a slightly hypnotic state.

[Audience Member: Do you have the egg wrapped with the black and the red beforehand?]

No. You do it after. Then we have a problem: we don't have some of the same furniture and technology to deal with this, so you guys are generally going to *bury* it. I think Brian mentioned that sometimes they crack it open to see what's inside. I've never seen that, but if you know of this, you may try it. What they used to do—and I think this is fantastic—is put it behind coal stoves or steam heaters, as it was a very dry heat, until the thing would just crumble. It would crumble to ash as all the moisture was evaporated out of it. That is a neat addition of the Fire Element to the practice. I haven't figured out *quite* how to do that—perhaps you guys could do it with hot coals? You want something warm and dry completely surrounding it. I'm just throwing this out there to you; you may find a way to do that.

[Audience Member: How do you know it's not fertilized?]

Hold it up to the light, you can usually see through it

even with candlelight. If you get eggs from a store, they're not supposed to be fertilized, unless they're sold that way. As a child I recalling seeing, occasionally, some blood in an egg, but I haven't seen that in years. Of course, I don't get organic eggs, either. I don't eat a lot of eggs.

[Audience Member: Even the organic eggs are not supposed to be fertilized.]

Yes. I don't think this is really a problem. People actually have to seek out the fertilized eggs because they want to hatch chickens, and that's a different market altogether.

So that's what you want to do. If you can find a way to create that hot coal or ash environment to cause it to dry out and dissolve faster, that would be fine too. We adapt. If I don't have a coal stove, but I do have either fire or a fire pit or a coffee can with ash in it, a sand bath essentially, any of this can work in some fashion—or you just bury it, and let it go back to nature.

We have two ways of purification in alchemy. The first is Fire—"going up"; it evaporates off. Purification through evaporation. The second is purification through filtration, meaning it sinks *down*, through the Earth. If you want to have pure drinking water, you can create a still of some kind to distill the water off out of the muck, or you can gravity-feed it through something, whether it be the Earth itself or whatever kind of filtration system you make. This is using gravity—the Earth is re-absorbing this and taking care of it. You bury it and the Earth takes care of it.

[Audience Member: I take it that happens slowly.]

Yes, that way is slow. That's why I think the Fire is a nice one, because that way you just get to the ash pretty quickly. In stories and letters that I have from folks who remember this as children, they've said they had no idea what was going on. They would be horribly sick; sometimes they would tie the healing of an illness to the dissolution of an egg. So in my mind, getting it over with faster is better, rather than later.

That's why I bring that up to you.

[Audience Member: Sometimes there's an element of speed involved as well. Something that's "speedier" is more cathartic as well. If it's an illness that's in its middle stages and you do some kind of Fire technique on the egg to "burn it off," it could go through a very cathartic process. My preference, unless you're at you're wits' end, I don't do that unless the client is healthy. Not that they don't have an illness, but they're hardy—they can take it. It's pretty dramatic if you've really tied that energy to the egg and put it to the Fire, it *goes*. Like in Chinese medicine, they don't deal with parasites until the person's in a healthy state, because the herbs that they have to use are so cathartic and so strong and so poisonous that a weak person, with parasites, they wouldn't deal with. They would build them up first, because they couldn't take the cure, it would kill them. Kind of like modern cancer treatment: it kills the cancer but it kills *them*, too. So it's the same thing with this. If they're not hardy, if it can still be effective burying it Earth and going at a slower pace, if they're not at a stage where, within a few months, it's going to be over with anyway, in that case you take your best chances.]

The advantage of having the old coal stove and the steam heat is that is took maybe twelve hours or a day, two days, depending on how hot it was. It didn't happen in a few hours. It was a slow, very dry heat that just slowly pulled all the moisture out of the egg, vaporized it, and then the thing crumbled.

[Audience Member: So, practically speaking, you could throw sand in your crockpot and stick it in there.]

That's right.

[Audience Member: When I did it, I just made a fire pit that I don't use for anything else other than this. I just make a fire and scoop a place in the corner that's just slightly below that level, so once the fire is burning and the coals are getting in there, I just take the drier ash that's insulating and put that in that little hole first, then I just put the egg in there softly, so there's no burning stuff in there yet. But the heat from the fire actually draws out the moisture, because it's insulated underneath. Like firewalking, if you've ever done it. It's the ash that's on top. It always looks horribly dramatic; they build up these huge fires, they break them down, but it takes hours to get it burned down to these beds of coals that they walk on. The ash actually insulates their feet. I'm not saying that there's nothing mystical or magical there—there is. But there is a certain amount of physical insulation that's there. So, same thing you can do with the fire pit. Really, the pit that I use is as big around as the diameter of my arm. Make a nice hot coal fire there. Dig out a little section just to put stuff that I want to be drawn. Build the fire first and burn it down a little bit, so there's some coals and some regular ash there. Take that ash and just drag the ash into the little hole, just to dry it. Then put the egg in there and build the fire up, strong.]

With that, keep in mind, too—this is something that you really need to grasp and wrap your heads around (of course, Gloria talks about it quite well)—the Earth is also a reflection of the corrupted state of the Shells, of the Qliphoth. These demonic forces are part and parcel of the Earth, in a way; these "sparks of light" from the collapse of the first Creation.

That's why ritual purity also involves keeping the hands and fingernails clean. In Kabbalah, they say that the Qliphoth enter through the dirty nails. An interesting point, because one lama told me a story—it's kind of neat, I was sharing this with Brian—how, if you're talking to a demon, it's kind of like the way we look at having coffee. He was saying, "You wear your rings on the ring fingers, one ring on each, because they enter through this part of the body—the hand. You know what happens if it comes in? We tie it off with the red thread and we bind it and then we interrogate it to find out what its name is and whatnot." [laughter]

Well, I told him, that's pretty neat. Thank you. [laughter]

That's part of it, too: the purity. The Earth, of course,

receives and purifies our excrement, our waste—all of our bad actions, all of our bad thoughts, and our physical waste. It's where our bodies return after they've been spent. In that way, you make an offering, if you want, of this egg and its disease to the Hell realms, to the demons, because, for them, that's food. They like that stuff. You don't; what they like, you don't. "Here it is—you can go away now. Don't bother us anymore."

If you do bury it, if you have an area that you use, the corner that you would use is the *northeast* corner. I can't necessarily tell you why that is. I know it's that way in several traditions, but I haven't gotten a very clean answer on that.

The other things that we do for purity are Fire and Water. This you're already familiar with. The prayers of Fire and the prayers of Water are often taken from the *Chaldean Oracles*. You've heard them in some of the rituals of the Golden Dawn. You also know the Aspersion Ritual that Joe Lisiewski talks so much about—you know it well, there's no reason for me to go over it.[2] That's a very useful ritual either *daily* or for special occasions such as preparation of a space. Maybe you're looking to do a healing with someone with this egg; you can do this as a preparation. You don't have to.

At this level, the operations of magic are very free-flowing. There aren't a lot of hard and fast things; it's principle-based rather than technique-based. It's what you as an experienced practitioner are bringing to it, and you know that from your own life.

Look at yourself. What are you really good at? Yoga, massage therapy, acupuncture—you know some folks that are just *so* good! They're *minimalists*. They're going to come in and do something really amazing with almost nothing, because it's *what they bring*, rather than what they do.

Of course, you can use incense with the Fire as well. If you

---

[2]See Joseph C. Lisiewski, Ph.D., *Howlings from the Pit: A Practical Handbook of Medieval Magic, Goetia & Theurgy* (Tempe, AZ: Original Falcon Press, 2011) 48-52.

are going to use incense, we suggest that you use *pine*. Pine is very energizing. Church incense is good. Unfortunately, the most common incense for keeping the boogeyman away—and they used to put it in little red bags and wear it around their necks—is *asafoetida*. I remember a couple of old guys—they were funny—they would say how their mothers would put it in these bags and make them wear it. And they said, "*Nothing* would want to get near you if you're wearing *that* stuff!"

I remember the first time I asked someone what it smelled like and he said, "Gym socks." [laughter] I have *not* brought any, by the way! [laughter]

[Audience Member: If it's burned, it's instantaneous.]

It's foul.

[Audience Member: It's foul. If it's burned it's like you can't go near it. You can't be in the chamber. Keep *everything* away from it.]

I think it's a digestive aid, but, regardless, with this, I remember Joe once said to me: "I can't understand this *asafoetida*. It seems like they just *love* that stuff!" And I said, "Yeah, well it *smells bad*! Theoretically they *should* like it, rather than going away from it."

So I'd be terrible with burning it in an operation. I'd have something else on hand just in case that goes south.

[Audience Member: Sure. But I've seen it in several texts. If things go south, forget everything else—that's your cut-and-run. Throw it on the coals, and it's instantaneous. Seal off your place for about thirty days!]

[laughter] With this also, again, is ritual washing. Washing before you do things and many prayers for that. You can also use ritual washing of a patient in the same way that you've used the egg. That's trickier, because it's the *water*, and the water tends to get messy, and go places, and you don't want that kind of water sitting around your house. So you would only do that in a running stream or someplace where you don't have to worry about the water. I need to make that very clear to you.

The last thing you want to do is, if you were to do some experiments, some ritual washing with someone for purification and then give that water to your plants! You don't want to do that.

Incense, of course, we can use a variety of purifying incenses, depending on the need or what you're used to or what you have available.

And then, of course, there is the air that we breathe. You yourself breathing, getting the individual who is not well to breathe—all of this is important. Having fresh air moving through. We don't breathe, we don't live—it's that simple. Air is the carrier of this energy. These airs literally move through us and fill us and expand us. That's why Air is so synonymous with psychic energy itself, because there is such a relationship between them.

Along with this we also use prayer. Prayer comes from the Latin *precarius*, "obtaining by begging," and the word *precari*, "to entreat." The most common forms of prayer are *petitionary* and *intercessory*, but we also look to others: *confessionary* (confession of one's sins), *lamentations* (prayers made in distress asking for release), *adorations* (honor, praise, and thanksgiving; expressions of gratitude). All too often we don't do the last two—we just call on these forces when we want something or we're desperate.

It's important that these prayers have meaning to you and that they be *short* and *to the point*. In fact, in *The Cloud of Unknowing*, a fourteenth-century manuscript, it states:

> A man or a woman who is suddenly frightened by fire or death is driven hastily and by necessity to cry or pray for help. And how does he do it? Not surely with a spate of words; not even a single word of two syllables. Why? He thinks it wastes too much time. So he bursts out his terror with one little word: *Fire!* Just as this little word stirs and pierces the hearts of the hearer more quickly, so too does a little word of

one syllable, when it is not merely spoken or thought, but also expressed with the intention of the depths of spirit, it pierces the ears of the Almighty God more quickly, than a long psalm churned out unthinkingly. That is why it is written: the short prayer penetrates Heaven.[3]

You'll see that most of the short, daily charms that are used in folk magic *rhyme*, because in their rhyming and in their repetition, they penetrate our subconscious. They put us in a receptive, hypnotic state. More importantly: *it gets right to the point*. The prayer gets right to the point!

That said, we have three types of prayers. You will see some work with the Psalms. We have spontaneous prayer, which we just mentioned. We have also specialized charms.

Another way of healing is—and here I should have mentioned previously the use of salt. Salt is also added to the water, usually—not always, but if you have it, add it. Salt is also used in dwellings to seal them. The way it's done is you would lay it across thresholds—doorways, windows. I've seen circles of salt. The theory is—and I think it may be true—that salt is kind of *caustic*, because it is caustic to us. It's caustic to whatever touches it energetically.

One of the things they would trap is to a spirit—a strange idea, a strange practice, if you think about it, but you need to put yourself in the perspective of the being which is (in this case) always hostile, to some greater or lesser degree. The entity is very chaotic; it's seeking to find some kind of center, it's seeking to do something. It's so emotionally overdrawn that it's perspective is very limited. It's very much like the vision that you see in movies, when they show someone who is under the influence of some kind of psychoactive substance—everything's kind of blurry, and there's tunnel vision. That's

---

[3]Anonymous (trans. Evelyn Underhill), *A Book of Contemplation the Which is Called the Cloud of Unknowing, in the Which a Soul is Oned with God* (London: John M. Watkins, 1922) 191.

really the kind of experience that they're having.

These beings that you say prayers to in the offerings—and praying *for*, not just praying *to*, but praying *for*, that's very important—they perceive the universe differently than you do. Which means that they perceive *light* differently than we do. It's often said that as you go to different levels on the Tree, things become brighter and more intense—and that's true, because things are just that. They're brighter. There's nothing filtering it out.

It also becomes more abstract. So it goes: brighter, brighter, brighter, more abstract, to whatever.

The reverse is true, too, that in the worlds below ours things are *darker* and more *concrete*. They're more *crunched in*. On one hand, we talk about why you do the Triangle of Manifestation—the Triangle of Art—and that's to *contain* these things, because not only do they *want* to be free, but they *hate* being free. "I won't to be free because it's so restrictive here..." But then, there's no focal point for them; it's too much of what they "want." That's why you generally don't play with those things.

The notion here is that the salt is somewhat caustic to them. You can somehow trap them in these jars, and salt will be in it. You put a lid on it. The notion is that it's a kind of gaseous, immaterial thing, and it's taking on a location in your time and space dimension. If you can't sense it here, rather than over there, then it's not in your time-space. So it's beginning to take on some kind of "corporeality"—a *density*, more and more dense than our world. With that, you can "catch" it, almost as if you would catch smoke, for lack of a better word. This salt is something very unpleasant to it. Afterward, you take the jar somewhere and get rid of it.

Salt is something to keep quite a bit of on hand. Don't leave home without it—better to have too much than not enough. I like sea salt myself, although for blessing places I like to use rock salt, which you can just drop into corners.

[Audience Member: Have you ever used black salt?]

No, I haven't. I know folks who, when they travel, they usually salt the rooms in their hotels.

The other one is *breath*—you can *blow* it away. Blowing, you know—"mommy, kiss my boo-boo."

[Audience Member: If you put this in a jar, and you've gotten rid of it—put it in your neighbor's yard—]

[laughter]

[Audience Member: —and you've never opened it...]

Yeah, you're kind of in a tough place there. I think that, eventually—

[Audience Member: It dissipates?]

—it figures a way out. That's my guess. That the containment is only temporary. The confusion is only temporary. That's my guess.

Which explains why—as you know, they see things very darkly. In fact, one can argue—and I think there's some truth to this—that in those realms things are very *dark*, and the only colors they perceive are dark reds and black. Whereas, when you move up, we perceive all this color; in your dreams, things are brighter, or things increase in brightness. For them, it's just the opposite.

Each realm has its area of vision or field or color of vision. They say some animals basically just see black-and-white, I'm told. They don't see a lot of color. Then you have others that just have *fantastic* night vision. Each of these is still an expression of a very narrow range of perception, somewhat specialized. That perception of sight represents the perception of *feeling* as well. The feelings are dark and heavy. Here, our feelings are (hopefully) lighter and more expansive. Very simple.

[Audience Member: So you're not opening the jar.]

You're not opening that jar! [laughter] Hopefully you're never going to need to do that.

Of course, then there's laying on of hands, which you know from all of your therapeutic touch methods. It's almost not even worth going over, but we call it "laying on of hands." It comes under the area of specialization known as *mesmerism*, or magnetic healing, which was very popular in the eighteenth century. The notion is that there's an energy that actually passes from human beings and can be used to help one another. This energy can be collected, by the way. It can be stored in "buckets." These were special kinds of "baths" that they used, which had water and steel rods put in them to channel it. Sometimes they called it "od" or "orgone"—whatever you want to call it. Much the same thing. The idea is that it can be condensed.

This is very important because we too often think of the spiritual world as too "abstract." But at this point what we are talking about is one of incredible overlap.

So any type of healing touch that you have, coupled with prayers would do. I have seen very ornate healing methods of the hands that are always the same way. They always do the same thing: moving the hands from top to bottom, sweeping away; moving the hands from front to back, sweeping away. All from the center out. Always the same thing. And again the idea is that you are pulling away, pulling away, pulling away—like wallpaper.

What some will do, is we will say, what happens when you do this? And this is neat because I have both felt it and not felt it. It is kind of peculiar. So you are going to have to see how this goes for you. I know one person who used to do it, and they used to actually kind of feel it on their hands and they would throw it into this bucket of water. Then they would get rid of the water. I do not feel that too much. I do not feel that stickiness too much, but I have on occasion, so I just mention that to you. And that goes back to the notion of contagion.

I do not believe that when you do healing, that there is really that much of a possibility of contagion. I simply do not. Because you are at the higher battery level, and if you are not then you should not be doing this to begin with. But I am open to the possibility that it can and does happen.

One of the ways you fortify yourself against this is just by getting rid of it. And that is why washing very well prior to and after healing is so important. Again, your sink is great for that because the water just goes out to the sanitation authority. They take care of it. So again, ritual cleansing, ritual healing and cleansing are all interconnected. And these sweeping motions, the notion, along with this is breathing. Lots of breathing on your part; holding it, pushing away. [audible rhythmic breathing]

They say prayers, and always at the end of it pray to the Father, Son, the Holy Spirit, Amen. Amen. Amen. They blow on the person, and as they blow the idea is that they are blowing away or scattering, penetrating and scattering, any remaining illness, disease, contagion, whatever it might be. This moving of the head and blowing is extremely important, and it is done in the sign of the cross. I believe this acts as a kind of a psychic seal, or imprint, on it. This is my belief.

So for example, you may come to me and say, "I have this pain in my shoulder, could you help me with it?" "Yeah sure, we will do the full [inaudible]." So I have you sit down. Relax, put the hands in the back, stand behind you. Put my hands on your shoulders. Stand behind them. Reassure them. Relax.

You know what? Let us say some prayers. Say them silently with me, or you say them out loud. [long pause] "Dear God, Father of us all, who has created man and woman in the most perfect state of health, who has sent thy son Jesus Christ into the world to heal all ills. And through the power of Holy Spirit has given his apostles and disciples the power to heal in his name. Be here with us now and bestow the same grace upon us. That our friend and child here may be healed of all infirmity, and made whole again."

You see how it is all linked? Do you understand how it is linked? Do you see the formula involved? The procedures? We will make a little aspersion. We will take some oil. These guys were not rich, they usually used olive oil. The head, the hands, the feet. Now we are tactile. We have had our prayers, auditory. We have sitting, so its also somatic. We have the oil, so it is tactile as well. And of course you are going to be getting a little visual stimuli as well. You do not want a bucket of water. I will take the egg. Maybe I will just mumble some prayers, or just hum a little tune, whatever puts me in a nice state.

[Mark is physically demonstrating a technique; humming.]

And drawing it out. We do it for a few minutes. We do it once. We wait a few minutes, maybe five, maybe ten, then you go back and do it again. You always do it three times. Always three.

I then take it, [the egg]. I wrap it in my red and black yarn or thread. And put it in a container off to the side to be carried out. Say a prayer: [long pause] "Dear Lord, thank you for your ever present power in the healing which you have bestowed upon all beings. Remove sin, error, sickness and death from this world, and restore us to that primordial state, as promised in your prayer, 'Thy Kingdom come, Thy will be done.' Amen."

Then we take it out, and we get rid of it. Now maybe we do not have an egg, but we do the same thing with the hands. That is, you have to clearly understand or visualize what it is you want to do, because your mind is the interconnecting force between the two. And you also have to have clear confidence that this was working.

So you do it once, you do it twice, you do it three times. It is that cyclic repetition that helps it sink in, and get absorbed by the other person. Do you understand the importance of the repetition? It is very, very important. It helps it get past your psychological barriers.

Repetition, repetition, repetition, is what trains the subconscious mind, because we are creatures of habit. And what you are doing is communicating to their mind, to them, really. You are bypassing their little rational guardian. You are communicating emotion. That is why everything is kind of dramatic. It is really a skill; it is an art. Rather than a formula, it is an art, of communicating, touching, directing, even distracting, so the message can go in.

It is not simply a matter of hypnotic suggestion. Although, that plays a key role in it. Suggestion is everything by the way. Suggestion is just a matter of belief, but it is also the fact that you have to be engaged in really moving that energy. If you can feel it moving, that is good. If you cannot, that is okay too, as long as you are confident that it is working. You can do this three times. If you need to come back again, come back and do it three times. Some people heal very quickly, some do not. Usually you will find it will be fairly quick.

Again, at that case, I may decide that as I am pushing this away, I do not really like the feelings, so I then throw the energy. When we are done we say the prayers. Again, as I said, I thank the lord, I dump it out, and then I wash up. All of this until you are feeling good. And with that of course you can use maybe some incense that is pleasant to them, you do not have to. These folks were not rich; they often did not. But there might be something that they enjoy, some essential oil diffusing. Anything that enhances the environment, relaxes them: rosemary is a great one to have, frankincense is a great one to have, rose oil. I do like sandalwood but it is a bit overused, so I think that the psychological impact is lessened by that.

[Audience Member: You said rosemary, frankincense, and rose?]

Yes. And as you anoint them too, again remember you would say prayers over the oil too ahead of time, and we will talk about some of those. And then after you are done with the sweeping, you can blow on the spot. [sounds of blowing] It is auditory, it is somatic, it is emotional, it is grabs them. And while this sounds like simply psychological tricks, they are just the doorway. Psychological tricks are the doorway. Do not ignore the doorway, otherwise you have to bust through the wall. And taking a sledge hammer to your own or someone else's psyche generally does not work out well. Everyone has a guardian of the threshold, or a bouncer. We want to make him our friend. [chuckling]

And he says: "Oh, dude—a twenty folded isn't gonna do it!" [laughter]

[Audience Member: Mark, when you do the cross on them, does it have to be in a certain place, or—]

No, you always do it over the body part.

[Audience Member: Over the body part that's being worked on or healed?]

Yes.

✿

Seal of the Brass Vessel

◇ PART FOUR ◇

At one point, some practitioners (and this would be fairly common in rural communities, particularly in southern or southeastern Pennsylvania) might just perform healings in their living room or in their sun room. Others might have a more formal practice area, with things that inspire around. It is nice to dress it up. We like that; the symbols have meaning to us.

I have seen some guys who have nice things: their old mirror, or an old desk that they keep their stuff in, a collection of brown and blue bottles and all sorts of things. All of it is mostly "just" for psychological purposes—but there is no such thing as "just." It is important because it inspires the people who come for help. You may not want that. You may do something else. You may actually know what all the stuff is for that you have. It does not matter as long as the environment that you create is conducive. Some people would travel and do it. All different approaches. But I gave you that general idea and it is important for you to work with it.

There are talismans and amulets that are often made for healing. Among the most famous is the SATOR Square. It dates back further than ancient Rome. I had someone tell me that it was possibly a very old magical square, far older than we often give it credit for. But that does not matter. What matters is that we have it, and you can still see it in use today. I have seen photographs of them in old barns. I have had people tell me they have found them carved into rafters in houses. And it is essentially a kind of defensive protective magic, protecting animals, buildings.

My great-grandfather even used it to heal rabies through consumption. I remember the first time I ever saw this as a child: it was written in pencil on a piece of paper, and it would be put between two pieces of buttered bread and the person would be forced to eat it. When you think about it, what do you hear in Revelation? "It was bitter in my mouth but sweet in my stomach." Again: connections.

Other times these magical items, whether they are words—which we'll talk about, how to make some—or phrases like this, would be written on a piece of paper, sometimes in ink even. And that must have been great for your teeth! They would put it in ink or sometimes in pencil or charcoal on a sheet of paper, a small piece of paper, and they would put it in water. Then they would hold their hands around the water, and blow on the water with their prayers. The person would subsequently drink it. The idea was that the charge of the amulet would go into the water and the person would ingest it that way. This is really no different than notions of crystal therapy. We call it "hydrotherapy": different kinds of healing with water, a very common practice.

I encourage you to work with that; I really do. It is something that is very fast and easy to do and often underrated. Some great experiments were done at McGill University (I think it was in the seventies) on healing energy and water. I wrote about them in the book on alchemy and in some other places.

Essentially the idea is this: "Let us see if the mind really has any affect on anything." So we get some water, and we are going to have three different people just hold it or do whatever they do with it. Get some psychiatric patients to hold it, and then some self-professed healers to hold it, and then just regular people. Then they would take it and they would put it on live plants. As expected, with the water from the psychiatric patients, for no apparent (other) reason, the plants would whither and die. The plants from the healers do better, and the plants from average people flourished in varying degrees.

So then they did it again, and they did it with seeds

soaked in a five-percent saline solution. The salt is going to inhibit any growth, so in theory these things should not grow. Of course, they did *not* grow with water from the psychiatric patients or average people but, surprisingly, they *did* grow from the healers. The healers actually could get these seeds to become sprouts even after they had been soaked in a growth-retarding solution.

So again, water is what we are made up of for the most part. Water is life. It is the closest thing related to that *pneuma*. We will talk more about that briefly when I discuss the *mist*, how this stuff begins to coalesce. It is in us. The water and part of that overlap—it is very important to give some attention to.

I would encourage you to make some of these squares on a Saturday preferably in the second hour of Saturn, although often we make them any time.

You can also make it on a Tuesday, that is a good day too. Just slap them up on your beams, under your doorways, wherever you want. These folks hide stuff, too. They hide them all the time. They hide them behind the sills and door frames. I have talked to guys who did reconstruction, renovation on houses, in Appalachia. We were talking about the stuff they find. The same thing about some of the guys doing old colonial houses, era houses down in the southern part of Pennsylvania and, I am sure, there are probably some here in the northern area. There is all sorts of stuff buried in the window sills: salt, mercury, mercury salts. What are you keeping away with *that*? [laughter] That is both a binder and an attractor, so you want to pull it in and then you want to keep it? [laughter]

Which brings me to the other point: do not play with mercury! Not just because you absorb it through your skin, but because it is a *thought enhancer*; it magnifies your thoughts. So if you have mercury in your chamber, or somewhere, please do watch your thoughts around it, and do not carry it with you.

It is indiscriminate, in that it will magnify your bad thoughts as well as your good thoughts. It does not care. I would just keep it in a cabinet, in a glass bottle with a seal, completely sealed, and away. And I only bring it out when I use it.

You can put it in a special box and put it away. Especially if it is dental mercury, which has been thrice distilled. Now, if you get mercury that has been distilled seven times, it would be considered philosophic or alchemical—that I would *really* treat with care.

You just put it in a glass bottle and you just keep it outside your normal range of presence.

Another thing they used to do which is quite fascinating—and I still see this done, a friend of mine has made a few—are *Himmelsbriefe*, or "letters from heaven." This is unique to folk magic; it is essentially a long prayer on a sheet of paper that people would have in their houses. I have seen them; these are wonderful to see, especially when they are in their old script and everything.

I have also seen more-or-less modern ones, above door frames in houses, which is kind of an extended house blessing. These *Himmelsbriefe*, if you can find them, are very nice collectible items, but more importantly they were so common that they used to print them up on a printing press. If you can have someone actually make one for you, it is an actual talisman, because it is a *written* talisman. It is a written blessing. They would carry them with them and all sorts of things. You do not see them much today, outside of a few locations, but this is part of the tradition, part of what was done, and a few people still do it.

You can do it as well; again, it is a prayer. You have the appropriate signs of the cross on it. The sign of the cross is important because it is always an equilateral cross, and often it is done three times; you see it written with: "Amen, Amen, Amen." Notice that *three* is the number—three times is a charm. The power of three.

[Audience Member: Could you say the prayer that the "letters" have?]

No, because they are anything; they are made up by each individual practitioner, and they are done by them. Sometimes they would be so popular they would make them up and have them printed up for distribution. I saw one that was done on an old blue mimeograph. That is more of a modern one, but you can find them as collectibles where they are actually letter-press from the nineteenth and early twentieth century. It is an extended prayer, written in the form of a letter. They are always carried on a person or displayed. They can be very simple or very ornate.

That gets us to written charms. There are often written charms that are to be carried on a person. These differ from the *Himmelsbriefe* in that they are shorter, more compact, and may not be intelligible to the reader, but are cryptic and clearly occult in nature.

[Audience Member: These Saturn squares, should they be made out of a particular material?]

They are usually made out of paper. In fact, what they used to do is carve them on wooden plates. The theory goes that you carve them on wooden plates and then throw them into a fire to start the fire. I have never seen that but I do know someone who did it. That was really neat. So just for the sake of consistency you can do it that way.

I have seen them carved into the wood with just a pocket knife, on a beam. I have seen them put on paper and tacked up there. I have seen them done with basically white paint or chalk on a wall.

[Audience Member: Would you put them in the South? West?]

You would put them in all four directions.

[Audience Member: I have seen them burned in with a brand as well, into the wood.]

Whatever is going to keep it there, that is the idea.

[Audience Member: The Saturn square itself, where would

you find it?]

You would find it in the back of Agrippa.[1]

For healing, you can also use teas, spagyric and alchemical work, or homeopathic. That is all acceptable. There is no particular emphasis that I have ever found in the [folklore on it] that was just part and parcel of it. The thing with the cross, whether it be written, done with the hand, done with oil, done with breath, is that it seals or fixes this desired state in the psychic body, and it imprints it in there, because the sign of the cross done that way is a symbol of equilibrium and protection. It is also a symbol of the Earth.

Sometimes pentagrams are used, but rarely. In these schools of magic, pentagrams are a symbol of power rather than protection. We think of the pentagram almost as a passive thing, like a shield; here it is a flaming and dynamic thing. It is raised. Energy comes out of the points of it, the rays. It is dynamic and vibrant, and that is a very different way to think of it.

There are other things which used to be done, and things to bless the house or bless an area. They would write on anything they had. They were usually done on smaller strips of cloth, and they were done in pencil, although I have seen a few done in other ways. They are really the equivalent of prayer flags.

This notion of writing your prayers on a scrap of cloth and tying it to a tree—whatever the sacred tree was in your area—was common in Europe up until about the tenth or eleventh century. This is one that I have for you.[2] It is pretty straight up. I made it more decorative than I normally do. They would just tie these onto a tree. Of course it is the same thing, that as the wind blows it carries the prayer, it carries the blessings, wherever the wind blows.

When possible, the Divine Names should be in red. Sim-

---

[1]See Donald Tyson, ed., *Three Books of Occult Philosophy* (St. Paul, MN: Llewellyn, 2000) 321.

[2]See image on facing page.

He that dwelleth in the secret place of the Most High shall abide under the shadow of the Almighty. I will say of the LORD, *He is* my refuge and my fortress: my God; in him will I trust.

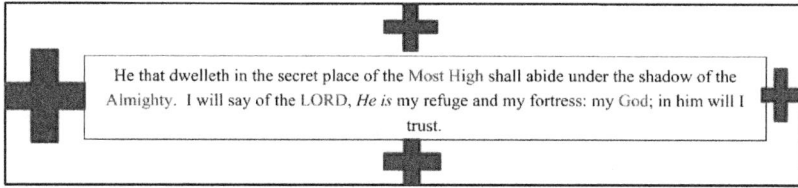

General Prayer Flag Design

plified "Greek crosses" or plus signs have been used. A dagger or obelus can be used suggestively for more defensive work of a mundane nature. In this regard it has a certain similarity to the dagger cults that moved from the Middle East into India and Tibet, giving rise to the Vajrakilaya practices, but the common "Iron Cross" design or *cross pattée* in some form is used. The cross is related to the notion of staking or fixing. This means to either interrupt or stop that which is undesirable or hold in place that which is desirable.

It is funny that we have this phrase, "A little bird told me." Language of the birds. The bird is the symbol of intuition, divine speech. The dove is the symbol of the descent of divine grace and illumination, but also, in alchemy, it is the raven and crow. The raven is a symbol of divine descent, both in Tibetan Buddhism, as a symbol of spiritual communication, and in the Nordic traditions I am told, because Odin's messengers are in the form of two ravens.

I know someone who used to write these and they would use an old quill pen (the feather). The techniques are very idiosyncratic when principle-based rather than methodological.

So this is linen,[3] which is nice because it will tear up really nicely. It will not last much more than a season or two. We have two colors again: we have red and black. The lettering is in red, because Fire is flaming. Fire is in a sense protection, but it is also sealing.

This is the opening phrase from the Ninety-first Psalm, and this is how things quickly got corrupted—as I write this with my pen here, the cloth is moving, of course. The Hebrew letters quickly get distorted. Make one mistake and you have made another letter. It stretches, too, when I am writing on it. You can see how quickly, in those days, it was very easy if you could not read what you were transcribing, you would not know it. Quickly the errors take place, and that is what made the *Sixth and Seventh Books of Moses* so interesting, because so much of it was just foully corrupted—and yet people were then using this corruption itself.

There is appended stuff in the back, which we will deal with—the third and the fourth appendices—which is very, very useful to us.

This is the first line of the Ninety-first Psalm with the divine name [El], which is Chesed: protection, mercy, grace, all of these things.

Generally those bags I gave you last time—they are called *Brauche* bags—are worn around the neck. I do not wear them around the neck. They are usually made out of red flannel, rather than white. These I made you because I could find these easily, but they are usually made out of red flannel—the color of fire; life, strength, vitality. As they wear it around their neck it protects the neck and the heart centers.

Very often what we do not realize is that they used to wear a lot of these talismans, on the different liturgical garments, to protect those psychic centers, or to help concentrate what they were focusing on, depending on the complexity of the act.

---

[3]Referring to the flag.

If you have a Bible, share it with a friend and open it up to the Ninety-first Psalm. If you have a pen, you may write it in red letter or black letter, whatever you like. You can mix it up, red and black.

You do not have to do it this way.[4] I have seen where they just write the words out and just a cross or two and that is it. I have taken the instructions that we see in the fourth appendix there, which shows you that for certain levels of protection the Ninety-first Psalm is considered the psalm *par excellence*. With that, the divine name associated with it is El, so it is just reinforcing what you have. Why do something different when you can just keep it simple and use what you've got, right? Why introduce more moving parts?

[Audience Member: Why reinvent the wheel, right? It is the same idea with the lineage. There are millions of practitioners in the past that have done it exactly this way. We can tap into that stream of consciousness. It helps.]

Then simply find a tree to tie them on, or take them with you and put them on your orchard somewhere. Put it on your own tree, also.

Now, you have to have your focus here when you do this. What is the purpose of this prayer? This amulet? This is for divine protection.

Not so much in the sense that you would do it if you think you are being threatened, but that to know that this divine presence is here and around you at all times, and that not only does it protect you in the sense that it keeps away unwanted influences, but it is also beneficial to you. That is what is particularly unique about this prayer when you read about it, that it is particularly beneficial, and confers a sense of optimism—optimism and good will and all of those wonderful joyful things.

You can put the cross at the beginning. You can put it at the end if you like, wherever there is a little bit of space. This

---

[4]Referring to the sample—see image on page 97.

is a practice you have to develop a certain artistic flair for. Whenever we are dealing with principles we have to develop a little bit of personal flair. Remember the purpose of this.

Now remember when we talk about these kinds of protective talismans, as we feel their importance, their value, and have confidence in them, these healing things generate beneficial states, and we are creating a healthy and clean environment for things to nurture and grow in. Our confidence in that, and our belief in that, has an energetic quality that is sensed by others and it is sensed by others who come into that environment and come in contact with it. You know it because you have experienced it yourself.

It happens whether we decide to do it or not. Just by your living and breathing and working in a certain space, you impregnate it with a certain quality. It is just the way it is. But here you are doing it consciously. "I really want this to be the quality here." In your house you have an overall quality you want to be present—but then again you have different ones in each room. The quality you want for your kitchen is not necessarily the same you want for your bathroom, not necessarily the same for your living room.

Look at the qualities you want in your house, and your environment. Your yard if you have one, or even your balcony if that is all you have, and say, "How is it that I can strengthen and reinforce those qualities of openness, of expansion, of well being, of health and wellness, all of those things?" That is where these kinds of talismans come into play. When we extend it beyond talismans, into actual interior decorating, then we are stepping into the domain of *feng shui*.

If you want to understand how this practice works in terms of interior decorating you should look at *Three Books on Life* by Marsilio Ficino. At some point we may talk about those, in which he details precisely the kinds of environments that are good for different types of personalities and different astrological signs.

There is only one edition I know of. It is in Latin with a

facing English translation.

[Audience Member: If you could just, so they can hear it from a different angle, talk about the relationship between faith and confidence, the feedback loop.]

The more we do things, the more confident we are. We know because we habituate ourselves to an outcome, whether it is playing the piano, the look we give our boss, or even how we sit and prepare to meditate. We habituate ourselves to particular outcomes. We are quite confident of what will happen because over time we know that "if this, then that." Everything in life is an if-then statement. Everything in life is cause and effect. Very often in our work we hear about faith and—how does it go? "Faith is the substance of things hoped for, the evidence of things not seen."

So we can have all this wonderful faith, but how do we do it? We *fake* it. We cross our fingers, click our heels, and hope it works—and that is okay, because in the beginning we have very little experience to draw upon. That experience we have to support in any way we can. As that experience grows we move more or less away from faith to *confidence*, which is a knowledgeable assurance of certitude.

Do you see the difference? I know that if I let go of this, it will drop. I do not even think about it. It is just going to happen. When we talk about faith, that is what we are talking about, that confidence, particularly born of experience, of the certainty of the outcome. If, then. There is no "but." It is if-then.

I want to talk a little bit about ritual exorcism, demons, and other psychic entities. In classical psychic physiology, as well as its later medieval and Renaissance descendants, various areas of the human body are ruled by planets, signs, and elements. These can be fairly simple in daily application, or more complex depending on the level of what the practitioner is seeing.

In addition, the twelve astrological signs and the thirty-six decans are given locations of rulership over the different parts of the body. This is derived through Egyptian sources, as you see in the ancient Egyptian text where it states the different gods going from head to foot, and what they influence, and that "Lord Tahuti ruleth over the whole of me."

You also see in medieval Renaissance astrology—the head starting with Aries, the feet ending with Pisces—the signs of the zodiac rule different parts of the body, and therefore influence the health of your body. Their cycles do, too. Planetary astral cycles of duality, as they spin and turn and interrelate, affect us on a microcosmic level, as we go through our cycle of living. This is the basis of medical astrology. This is the basis of alchemy. This is the basis of Culpepper's medieval medicine. This is the basis of much healing in folk magic.

In addition to the body being seen as a microcosm of the universe, the head and brain as well is seen as its own kind of microcosm within the microcosm. Without our head the body would not function, so the head has seven orifices, eyes, ears, nose, mouth, each given to a planet.

The brain has various major and minor divisions in it which were known by the ancients to affect the different parts of the body. They knew this. Not as well as we do, because we have better ways of understanding that through technology, but they were aware of it. Despite this, the brain (until the Renaissance) was seen as inferior to the heart, and that is very important.

When we talk about mind, we talk about the heart. When Egyptians talked about where we are located, it is the heart. Same as in other places, in the Orient, the heart is where the mind resides, not the brain. The Egyptians thought the brain was a useless piece of thing. They used to drain it out and throw it out. I do not necessarily agree with them but it is kind of funny!

Now with the heart as our center of consciousness, that is, our consciousness, but also spiritual consciousness and soul, intellectual functions were relegated rightly to the brain, as well as other material functions to the nervous system. The nervous system was in the domain of Mercury, messenger of the Gods, and, of course, Mercury is air, so the nervous system, it was thought, could be affected by breathing—how we emotionally respond.

The rulership of the brain in particular has always been given to the Moon, whose relationship to the Earth is kind of like a psychic twin. The Earth and the Moon are very intimately related. The power of the Moon over human physiology and behavior has long been observed and speculated about, and the Moon is both Watery and Airy. It is the ruler of night, of primitive magic, of dreams, of agriculture, in the sense of growing cycles, of health and illness, and of madness.

All of our deeply primitive, chaotic, and frightening aspects of creation were given rulership of the Moon. The Moon was sent to rule over you, creatures of the night, things of the dark, dimly lit, dimly [exposed]. For this reason, demonic evocation is an activity usually undertaken at night. The demonic forces generally fall under the domain of the Moon, although, as we said earlier, the kabbalists make it very clear that these forces are somehow deeply intermeshed into our material Earthly structure.

Again, these are a reflection of the inner state of the person. So when we look at nightmares, those things that scare us, what are we really looking at? What are they? What are our demons? Our fears. And what do our fears come from? What kind of thinking? Obsessive and compulsive, erroneous thinking. All the demons, these shells, these *qliphothic* shells, have the spark of the divine. All of the names in Hebrew have a divine "-el" or "-ya" attached to them to show that they are an extension of the Creator. They are not outside its domain or control or influence. There is something redeemable about them.

But they are *excess*. Why do we have excess? Because we are either clinging to something or rejecting something. Either I want more, or I do not want any—and what is that? Duality. Back and forth. All or nothing. It goes back to one of our most early experiences. One of our most early experiences is "I want what makes me feel good; I want to run from those things which make me feel bad." I do more of what I get rewarded for, regardless of what it is.

All of this is happening on a very deeply emotional level. There is very little rationale involved. That is why when we think of these angelic forces, we often think of them as kind of cold and aloof. Maybe they are in that sense, a little too rational. At the same time, when we need some assistance, where do we get it from? These on the other side, these so-called demonic forces, they are emotion. They are powerfully emotional. It is like having a wild animal. I do not like to make that comparison, but it is the closest thing I can think of.

Think of a time when you saw someone—and most people have not—but when you saw someone that was really out of control. The person that is really out of control seems to have no physical limits, because they do not have a body that controls them. Now, when I say "no limits," I mean that you cannot restrain them through normal measures. So what do they do? They feed off of energy. What is energy? What is your energy? Where does it come from? Your emotions. So if your emotions are fully anchored in compassion and altruism and openness and a true lack of ego-clinging, for lack of a better phrase, but instead clinging hard to that sense of who you are and what you are, then they are going to push your buttons, pull your fear out, and eat you, until you run away or something happens—because that is their food.

In fact, the worse it is, the better they like their food. It is an extreme—it is about extremes. Anything terribly toxic is terribly emotional or terribly powerful, which is nice when we get into the transformative side of things. It is wonderful. But we are not talking about that yet. That is something else. It is reasonable to suggest that demonic entities and demonic forces are unintegrated aspects of our psyche, individually and collectively, and that they also exist as psychic projections, as well as independent entities.

The idea that what we think of as demonic forces are "just" psychological projections of our unintegrated, infantile nonsense and obsessions is true, but thinking that is *all* they are is false. They are also external, objective entities, clearly of a very narrow and limited nature, though—limited and uncontrolled, it is just like a top spinning, bouncing off of us.

For the individual, the location of these forces can be seen in the head or brain, whereas the angelic forces can be seen to reside in the heart. That is a simplistic approach, but a good one. At the same time we have to look at these demonic forces, or what are labeled as them—again some of them are just what you think of as "evil." Others are not. They are more like psychotic. You have certain kinds of sociopathic personalities out there, that are highly functional, extremely functional and successful.

A lot of them are like that. A lot of them are: "It is all about me." That is the big point. What is that force, what is it all about? It is about "me." So when you are egocentric and obsessive and complaining—"I feel like crap! Maybe if I invoke this demon I will control it and it will get me what I want." Do not call me when that happens. You better be ready to write a real big check. We will make sure the lesson is learned.

It is reasonable to believe that upon death the psychic energies or channels get fired off. As the nervous system decays and degrades, the energy within it is being fired off, and this gives rise to different signs and sensations and different feelings in the body, in the mind as well. Our creative notions of heaven and hell get released at that time—most of it, for our concern, is a perception.

This is said all the time. I know Swedenborg said it; Boehme said it. You hear all these different teachers of different traditions saying it in some way: "We can make a hell of heaven, or heaven of hell. It is a matter of what we bring to it. It is a matter of our perception."

One of the great examples of Hell: a place where you have two people who have forks attached to these long beams attached to their arms so their arms cannot bend and they cannot feed themselves. What do they do? They starve to death. In Heaven it is the same situation—but they feed each other! So a lot of this is a matter of perception. I am going to talk to you about some of these perceptions, and what they are like in reality so you do not have a false notion.

It would be reasonable to suggest that, as a daily concern, what we think of as "demonic forces" would be purely subjective, but that is not always the case. There is a link to it and a vibratory connection, like [al-Kindi] talked about: the thread, the threads go out. Those act as an energy conduit, back and forth. I know this seems very literal; please do not take it that way. At times it seems that way because as it gets concrete it does get kind of literal, like a vibratory frequency, like a radio tuning in. It has to be tuned in somewhere.

You perceive what is a reflection of yourself. At some times, if you are having nightmares, it is very good. In fact, there are certain practices, which we have not talked about, which are specifically designed to induce nightmares. The reason for this is that by inducing fear, you get to overcome it. That is why often when you do these practices of evocation, you do it in not only a private place, but in a place that is desolate, so that the environment is conducive to the evocation of fear, because the only way to overcome that is through courage.

It is extreme. This is very extreme. You have to understand it in that way. A lesser way, of course, is through dream work, which is still equally terrifying. You just do not have to travel anywhere.

Now, something to know about is when exorcisms are performed for real—when it is actually decided that a person is possessed or plagued by an external entity. It is not neurotic. It is not a psychotic break. It is not make-believe. There is really an unpaid tenant in the dwelling—someone not paying rent, if you know what I mean. You will notice that it is the *head* that they constantly anoint. Right here, or here [indicating the crown of the head]. For most intents and purposes what we call the "third eye" is really an extension of the crown. They are one and the same. During the daily cycle of the energies, the energy comes in from the top and circulates around.

[Audience Member: So is it sealing?]

It is purifying. That is why you blow on it, too. That is why when you do the smoke purification, there is always the blowing. Because it is actually blowing it into the center, into the Middle Pillar. Whenever you are dealing with that, you are essentially dealing with purifying, essentially purifying the Middle Pillar. You have to get that energy all the way through—all the way down—to the feet. Out through all of the psychic channels of the body, pushing it out, because the central channel at this point is very constricted. You need to fill it and expand it. Extremely constricted, especially down low.

It has to be flexible. Clear, flexible, bright. Remember all of the positive qualities. Clear, flexible, bright.

Here is an interesting little piece that I picked up from a Khenpo: "It is generally said that if you know the origins and history of the worldly gods and demons they will no longer be able to harm you. The same holds true for a *rudra*, that is, a human that becomes a demon. You are behind their malignant effects once you understand the history of their origin and development. That is why I have gone into some detail into the origin and histories of this one."

What these particular types of demons do is they create obstacles to practitioners on the path. This one that he is referring to is particularly trying to get practitioners to break their vows. I think that is interesting, because in modern times the term for a "male witch" is a *warlock*; this comes from the eighteenth century by the way, and in Scottish it means an "oath-breaker."

Again: thought, word, and deed; do we keep our word? Can

I trust your word? The notion of these ideas of thought, word, and deed are multi-faceted and multi-leveled and intertwined.

The Element of Air is important because it is the airs which are confused or malignant to begin with. We need to create conditions that allow them to flow according to their accord back to a healthy state. Now, this is fascinating; I was never quite sure of this, but when they do an exorcism—and I have spoken to two Catholic priests who were official exorcists, and a Protestant minister who got thrown into doing one down in the bowels of Carbon County. There was always a reason I never liked that place. It is not quite Sleepy Hollow, but it is close!

It is interesting that they would always do them in the dark. One of the easiest things to do is to turn the lights on and open the windows. Get some fresh air moving in there. Why are you doing this in the dark? The reason was never quite clear. I think that is just the way they have always done it, but it is because that is [its] natural habitat, and that allows it to come up. By pulling it up they can deal with it, rather than letting it hide.

So when we talk about going into the dark places that scare us, this is not a metaphor. I want to make that very clear. That little phrase from *Return of the Jedi*—"I'm not scared!" "...You *will* be!"—is an understatement. Just keep that in mind. At the same time, you have to come to grips with these parts of yourself, and you can do it very well. The more you come to grips with these parts of yourself *within* yourself, the more you are able to come to grips with them *outside of* yourself. That is the key.

What happens is people screw up and they think they are going to go play *Ghostbusters*, and they are not prepared. They do something stupid to begin with. They get themselves or someone else hurt. Of course, they have to be pretty neurotic and unbalanced to want to do that to begin with. It just further throws them out. So we want to open the windows and get rid of stale air. Stale air is by its nature associated with illness and death. Fresh air, good diet, healthy foods; if the person is there you can try and get them to at least eat more vegetarian. You certainly do not want them eating too much meat at that time. And pleasant odors. All these things which make it unpleasant for our uninvited guest, while encouraging it to leave of its own accord.

The classical method of exorcism that the church uses is essentially a struggle, it is a battle. You do not want to do that. It is too devastating.

If we talk about this air, or this mist that becomes vaporous and condenses—some of you may have seen it in your work. It condenses, as we have said, into water, into our bloodstream. I mentioned on the way up a movie that I had watched on experiments of the afterlife, where these folks in England in the nineties did work on spiritualistic phenomena and manifestation. It was very interesting because they actually use a glass device which—as was told to them by the spirits they were communicating with—they were to use as a kind of condenser for the energy. Remember: this is airy and vaporous, so the fact that it is a glass device means the air is not moving outside of it. At some point it goes from very subtle energy to something that actually experiences boundaries. Until that is actually done, it is easily diffused.

They had basically their version of an "orgone energy accumulator," if you will—which is very similar, I noticed, to a device mentioned in one book on Solomonic magic. They had some very interesting phenomena take place. I think it is called *Experiments in the Afterlife* or *Search for the Afterlife*. It is about the Scole grope. Rupert Sheldrake was a part of that as well as the British Society for Psychical Research. That is why I mention it.

This cloud or mist often is seen as blocking the gateway to Eden. This is also the Cloud of Unknowing, the cloud of the path of the Devil, the cloud that led the Children of Israel, and the cloud that surrounds Jesus. This cloud is a condensed moisture formed by spinning actions that concentrate it. It is

an action of Air upon Water. Abbot Trithemius, the teacher
of Agrippa, states:

> The *Spiritus Mundi*, that is, the Soul of the World,
> resembles a breath, appearing at first like a fog and
> then condensing like water. This water was in the
> beginning pervaded by the principle of life, and light
> was awakened in it by the *fiat*, the will, the desire,
> the action of the eternal spirit. This spirit of light
> called the Soul of the World, or the Astral Light, is
> a spiritual substance which can be made visible and
> tangible by the art, that is, by magic, alchemy. It is
> a substance, but being invisible we call it spirit. This
> Soul, or *Corpus*, is hidden in the center of everything,
> and can be extracted by means of the spiritual Fire in
> man, which is identical to the universal spiritual Fire,
> constituting the essence of nature and containing the
> images and figures of the universal mind.[5]

There is a lot there. What it says is that there is an energy
that pervades everything. It is similar to the action of air upon
water. It has these resemblances. It is moist and it moves. It
permeates everything and therefore can be extracted from
everything. In its essence, it contains within it the spark or
the knowledge, or the imprint, or the blueprint—the genetic
material, if you want—of *everything*, which therefore can be
accessed. This is made visible. This is an invisible energy that
can be so tangible that it lights up. You can see it. We call
it the *aura*. Sometimes you see flashing lights, but it can be
condensed and made very full.

The spiritual Fire in each and every one of you is identical
to the universal Fire. It is constituting the essence of nature

---

[5]Johannes Trithemius, "Miraculosa," Chap. XIV, quoted in Franz
Hartmann, *Magic: White and Black, or The Science of Finite and
Infinite Life, Containing Practical Hints for Students of Occultism*
(London: Kegan Paul, Trench, Trübner & Co., Ltd., 1893) 213.

and contains all the images and figures of the universe. So as you meditate upon your spiritual Fire, that inner spark within you, it is the same as—it is identical with—meditating on (as we will call it) the Mind of God. There is no separation. There is no difference. You are in that image, made of it.

This light resides in the Water. It is hidden as a seed in all things. Everything that originated from the Spirit of Light is sustained by it and therefore this spirit is omnipresent. The whole of nature would perish and disappear if it were removed from it. It is the principle of all things. Everywhere. Everywhere. There is no place where it is not. We are, everything is, just a condensed specialized expression of it—of this energy, of this action, of the light.

Robert Fludd (the Rosicrucian mentioned earlier) believed that the human soul is said to reside not in the physical density of the body but rather in the cavities or the open spaces of the body, particularly the brain, because within that there are cavities and there are areas of spaces. Fludd, like his predecessors, gives the soul a vaporous or Air-like quality without necessarily calling it such. Again, the word spirit or *spiritus* means energy, life force, rather than what we think of as soul. Soul is more of our sense of self or self-awareness. The ancients said that the Earth supplies the body, the Moon the spirits or life force, and the Sun the soul.

Pythagoras—and Reuchlin—assigned the qualities of the supreme, superior, and inferior worlds to the three cavities of the body: the head, the chest, and the abdomen. We see this threefold system repeated over and over again. In the *Sepher Yetzirah* we see the three mother letters are given to the head, the chest and the abdomen. Fire, Air, Water—and yet what do we say, too? We have three different ways of processing information: sight/Fire, Air/auditory, Water/somatic or feeling.

We can tell from basic NLP or Neuro-Linguistic Programming whether a person is visual, auditory, or somatic-kinesthetic based on their breath pattern. If it is up high, and your eyes are big, you are Fiery. If it is low and slow and deep then it is very somatic. And if it is middling, the chest is moving, you are auditory, or Air. So this three-fold vision is not just something we can look at as separate but we can see it even in these practices.

Paracelsus said, on the blood, "the human blood contains an airy, fiery substance. And this spirit has in its center the heart, where it is most condensed in form and in which it radiates. And the radiating rays turn to the heart." This energy condenses; it radiates out; and it comes back. This life force is focused in our heart. The power of the light is said to be the size of one's thumb.

Those of you who may have studied Vajrayāna, if you ever get teachings on the tomb, or the inner fire, the central channel is the size of your thumb. When you visualize the deity, you visualize it the size of your thumb. Here it is the size of your thumb; this energy is roughly that big.

Paracelsus described this as the "dweller in the heart," and as a blue flame, equal in size to the last joint of the thumb. He says the heart is the seat of the microcosm.

Hermes states that the human heart is formed like a pyramid, and we often see the triangle associated with it. Here we have Yod He Vav He (יהוה), Yod He Vav (יהו) like a triangle, part of the heart, radiating out, and through these radiating rays are psychic projections in which the healing of mind and body are facilitated. So again: we started the day meditating on the heart. We end the day with this blue flame on the heart.

We start the day talking about how important it is to have these relationships to others, in a positive altruistic sense. Now we see why, because in essence everything is within us. If we dismiss something out here, we dismiss it in ourselves. But if we can transform it within ourselves, then we can transform it without. The error is in trying to change something outside *first*, rather than within.

What I would like you to do before you leave is to draw

the SATOR Square in your notebook.[6]

Remember, everything moves and moves fluidly. Air and Water form Mercury in the alchemical model that we use. So we are always using the Air and the Water—the material life, that is the energy. That is moving, that is everything that keeps you alive. In one area of alchemy, everything is said to be differentiated Mercury. So it is light, it moves, it is expansive. This is the sustainer of life. In fact I think *feng shui* means Air and Water, so that is Mercury. That is the life force. That is what we are working with.

[Audience Member: So when we are with someone we are using our energy?]

Yes—theirs, ours. You may use yours to jump-start it but you are pulling it from the environment. The environment is filled with it; there is no place where it is not.

[Audience Member: So you manipulate it with your focus and intent, and use everything that is around you?]

Yes, that is correct. It keeps your mind focused. You have to have something to concentrate on. There are a lot of different ways to do it, but let us keep it simple; as you progress you get better. I know some people who do not even do anything anymore. The just put their hands one or two places; they treat everyone the same way and they always get the same results because they have moved on. Until then, let us enjoy the variety and have fun.

I think that is why mirrors were sometimes used. The reflection of light off of a mirror was said to confuse demonic spirits. And I always wondered about that. I think the reason is that flashing light is too bright. They are so used to dark things. I talked to some folks that are far more experienced in that than I, and that was their rationale.

⚜ ✳ ⚜

---

[6]See page 114.

S	A	T	O	R
A	R	E	P	O
T	E	N	E	T
O	P	E	R	A
R	O	T	A	S

The SATOR Square

◇ PART FIVE ◇

We'll get started. A typical small talisman that one might make—sometimes called a "charm"—can be written out on paper. One example says on it: "Beneath thy guardianship I am safe against all tempests and enemies. JJJ." Well, who's "JJJ"?[1]

Yod, yod, yod (ייי). What do three "yods" represent? The Holy Trinity. Why is it "J"? Is there anyone who can tell me?

[Audience Member: Because of the...Latin change in alphabet?]

"I" and "J" are the same, and this would have been out of German, "Jehovah." Okay? Now, I have little quotation marks around it. Someone said, "What's that?" A quotation mark. I just put it up there to confuse you, because you come up and say, "I want to write this down and I want to get it right." I look at every mark that's on there—I better put those marks, because THAT's there, and this mark, because THAT's there. Right? [sounds of assent]

I just put them there to make you do that, so you can understand some of the problems and the procedures in what goes on when you transmit information from one generation to another—which just means from one person to another. *Without* modern technology. If you don't know what "JJJ" means, you may mistake it for something else. It doesn't necessarily mean it's horrible if you think it means "James Jesus"

---

[1]The present discussion with audience members has been transcribed "as is" for the sake of demonstrating part of the point of the lecture, *viz.*, how and why "errors" creep into magical formulæ, as well as the detail with which one ought to study them for the purpose of generating a sound subjective synthesis.

or whatever. Not horrible—but that's not what it means. And why is "yod" also used? What is "yod"? Those are the little tongues of fire, and the first letter of the Tetragrammaton.

Now, the amulet which you have—and the long one which I've asked you to write out—was one which one of my great-aunts carried within her wallet. Oh, this is a nice one. There's so many of them. We haven't even scratched the surface in the last day. We have not even scratched the surface—there are so many things we need to try and cram into the next few hours. Remember, I wrote it out, and I put it over there, and I said, "Now make yourselves useful and write this down. And as soon as you're done, pass your written copy on to someone else, so they can copy it. The front of this—this is on two sides of a piece of paper—front, back; front-side, back-side. And it reads: "An amulet to carry on your person. Carry these words with you and no one will be able to assail you." Now I've printed in block letters: "AGANIA, AZARIA, MISAEL." [spells out previous three words] Now, of these three, what do you think they are?

[Audience Member: Angel names?]

Right. Why do you guess that?

[Audience Member: The "-el" on the end.]

Yes. The "-el" is the only thing that gives it away, that they are angels. If you go to look these up, you'll only be able to find "MISAEL." You will find parts and pieces of the previous two. Meaning what?

[Audience Member: They have different names? Or they were transcribed or written down—]

It was a transcription error. Now, you'll find pieces of them, you'll have the roots of them—but that's what happens. You still write it out as it is. "Praise ye the Lord, for He has kept us from Hell, and rescued us from death and preserved us from fire." What is that reference to? "Preserved us from fire." What is that in reference to?

Nebuchadnezzar. "They threw the three men into the fires, and I saw a fourth walk against the—walk amongst them, with the brilliance of the Sun." [general sounds of understanding]

"They are four." Notice it has a semicolon there, rather than a comma. Probably a transcription error. "They are four. May the Lord present the fire against us, from whom adversities—" and then it's "N-point-R"—"Prince of Peace, and all manner of contention"—power, contention—"power is protection for all who carry this blessing with them." That is awkward.

It is probably a translation error. "The Lord present the fire against us, from adversities." Now: "present" is actually "protect us." The Lord protect the fire against us from adversities.

"Prince of Peace and all manner of contention. Power is protection for all who carry this blessing with them. N. R." ("N. R." like "Nazarus Rex.")

"All manner of contention." And the contention—the reading is that the very thing has turned against itself. The very thing has turned against itself. Back side: "They will possess a GRAND SECRET—" 'grand' and 'secret' are both upper-case— "which no other being understood. Christ is in the midst of peace, went with his disciples." Now, "is in." I purposely put that in there. Because in the original, the last letter was very slurred. And I made a note to myself to check, to see if that was an "S" or an "N." And if you were to read that, which would make more sense?

"In the midst of peace." Right. So make a correction there— make your notation so that that should be "in the midst of peace." "Went with his disciples abroad." St. Matthew, St. Mark, St. Luke, and St. John.

"Christ in the midst of peace went with his disciples abroad. St. Matthew, St. Mark, St. Luke, and St. John." Always going to be those four. "The four evangelists protect me—" and here you put the name of a person, if it's someone else. Many people also put their own name there. So you would say: "The four evangelists protect me," for example,

"John." Okay? Sometimes it was even written more strangely, because of the maternal line. It would always be something like, "Protect me, Frank, the son of Barbara." You [hear] it? Okay? [sounds of assent] Comma. "The ever-praised majesty and unity of God. J 'period' J 'period' J 'period' Amen." Then beneath it: "quote" "dot" "dot" "dot" with me at all distances "period" Amen "period" "quotation". Then you have three things beneath it—three dots, three "J's", three "yod's". Now I put that there because on the original it was three dots. [And] I put that in my notebook as a reminder to me to tell you that whenever you see those three dots it's also the same as three J's which also is the same as three yod's.

So, get rid of the J's and the yod's if you don't want to use them—the three dots are on the original. Or make a note on your paper that the three dots are the original. You just have one of them, not all three of them. Now, you see how easy it is to make a mistake. [sounds of assent] You get it? I really want to bring that home. Because we do a lot of work and we have taken it for granted that someone's going to hand us a photocopy or send us a PDF. That just wasn't done. And just a simple slip of the pen and somebody's writing something else down—is it "is" or is it "in"? My notes to myself suddenly become, for you, part of the package. My marginalia suddenly gets incorporated into the thing. So we have to have a bit of sympathy when we think about the earlier transcriptionists and the burden that was placed upon them.

Now, again, this is just one of many, many kinds of amulets that would be made—as you can see, they were different, they weren't the big, symbolic amulets that we think of or talismans that we think of in ceremonial magic. These were written—these were words. Sections of scripture are said to be holy in and of themselves. So the Bible was looked upon as a magical book itself. If you open up some modern books on Buddhism or Kabbalah (such as by Godwin), you'll notice a little statement at the beginning of the book. It says: "This book contains sacred images or sacred texts. Don't read it in the bathroom." [chuckling] Why's that?

[Audience Member: Because you're supposed to be clean when you touch the Word of God and wash your hands before you open the Bible.]

[Audience Member: There's a feng shui reference for that as well, which is "anything you don't want, you flush away." So—]

That's right.

[Audience Member: It's an old technique. We've talked about that before—any bad correspondence, anything that we don't want—what do we do with it? Put it on the back of the toilet, on the tank, and every time you're flushing the toilet you're draining that energy out. So if you're reading it while you're doing your business then whatever you're getting rid of there, that energy, that water will—you know water, we've already talked about it already, water really condenses and holds that etheric charge, so you're doing that, you're charging yourself up with the water, that cold water is pulling it down and the flush is draining it away from you. So you don't want that to be the case.]

It's a distinct sense of a lack of sacredness. You know the notion of original cleanliness is important in the beginning of all work. Later on you have some "wiggle" room. But you don't get that "wiggle" room in the beginning. Because you have to begin to understand the nature of physical and psychological cleanliness and how they all work together. How they overlap. Earlier we said everything was what? Thought, word, and deed. So you just write the material it says on the front side. You don't write "on the front side" or "amulet to carry on your person." Now, you could. What might have happened is you might have to say to someone just to remind them because they're a little dense, "an amulet for carrying on your person" you sent to them in the mail, to remind them, and then what will happen is someone will pick that up and that will now become part of it, as they—

[Audience Member: The other thing is—and I've done this in the past—is used the same one for an act of charity, which is—you spend a lot of time, I make up a really nice one, I tie it off, and then I leave it some place discreet, for someone who ever needs it to find it.]

[Audience Member: They pick it up and they read it, they open it. If they're so inclined—to see, then it says "an amulet to carry on your person, for protection."]

Drop it off at the local laundromat. Where it says "front side/back side," that's just directions.

If we had time I might show you how to do the triangular ones. Reduction—reduction talismans. Now, with this—[long pause]. So write that out, carry it on your person, make it nice, and there you have it. Give them out as Christmas gifts or something—whatever you'd like. The other one is simple, as we've mentioned—but the important part that we also have is everything is that we say "thought, word, and deed." Prior to any significant magical act—I don't like the word "magic," by the way. I really don't. We need to realize that there is three, sometimes four, principal areas that need to be understood in preparation. This is part of the notion of purity. Of cleansing, of "getting rid of," which we call under the general heading of "exorcism" or "getting rid of things from ourselves." We do that through prayer, fasting, and alms. Those are the three. Prayer, fasting, and alms. A fourth one is sometimes added, which is "confession." Confession needs to be done verbally. Out loud. Not simply to yourself. Ideally it has to be done to another person. So, those of you who come from a Catholic background are vaguely familiar with this notion of "confession." If you're not Catholic, then you can say your confession to someone else. If not, you just have to say it out loud—but it has to be a sincere statement regarding where you have erred, where you have done wrong, and the statement that you will not do it again. It's really that simple. Don't be "sorry"—don't do it!

As I stated to you last night, in those days, the notion of "seminary" didn't occur until after the Protestant Reformation. That was a response to the Protestant Reformation. Being a priest up until then was an apprenticeship; you were apprenticed to whoever the local priest might be. You learned from them, so it was an apprenticeship relationship. That's how you learned liturgy, that's how you learned the rules of the day, that's how you learned to read.

It's one thing to say, "You know, nobody's perfect! We all make mistakes!" Well that's true. But what's your point? It's important to recognize where you have made a mistake *and not to do it again*. Sometimes those are big ones—sometimes they're just small ones. As we go further and further on the path, the big ones get ground down, they get sanded off—but the small ones remain. Those are the ones that trip you up like a pea in your shoe. It's very amazing how the small ones can do the worst damage. We say, "it's just part of the human condition." We recognize it and then we don't say or do that again. At some point it becomes: "I won't think that again." I will not think it—and when it comes up we simply let it go. Rather than clinging on to it and making a big deal out of it and driving ourselves nuts.

Concerning prayer and fasting and alms, there was a time before anyone took the Eucharist when they fasted. The Orthodox still do that. I don't know if the Catholics do, but the Orthodox do. Some of the old Lutherans used to. It's very good to fast, to give your body a rest, and to deprive it a bit, because then you just get to see how habituated you are to things. Alms, of course, is generosity. Get rid of your stinginess and greediness and selfishness.

Very important to undertake these. Very simple, very straightforward, very important. Now, I don't have time to go over as much as I'd like; there are many things unsaid. So—does anyone have any questions on anything that we did yesterday?

Regarding prayer flags, we didn't call them "flags." We

just made up a name for them—we just write them on these things and tie them. They had a formal name for it.

[Audience Member: Did you hang it on a tree?]

Yes. But they used to have a special tree for this. I've seen them just put outside buildings; I've seen them tacked on. Probably just to keep the birds away when they plant, you know. On tomato stands, you know. You go up and it has all this stuff written on them. They're written in pencil.

Well—they formalized the practice. They formalized the whole practice, in a way. This practice probably thinned out somewhere after the twelfth century. I mean, it didn't really, because you'd always see stuff like this tied to flags or tied to banners. It holds over, but the common practice of this, you'd see a lot.

Now, we talked about trapping negative energy in jars. We talked about getting rid of it (or keeping it out) with salt. We've talked about getting rid of it with blessing and prayers and extracting it with an egg. How to take care of that egg after you've gotten rid of it, because we believe contagion plays a role here. We've talked about offerings, and how they're—

[Audience Member: Can you demonstrate how you wave the egg over the body?]

You rub it.

Always very simple. It's always from top to bottom, from inside to out. So always—top to bottom; inside, out. Always that way, because you're moving it out the extremities. The idea is that the energy flows out the arms, the feet, and you want to move it down. You physically touch them with it, and you may hold it there, too. You might even hold it there and move it around. Develop a little rhythmic sensation there. Part of it is that you have to develop your own natural style with some of this. That's why we're dealing with principles rather than formula.

[Audience Member: The egg usually ends up with a person's temperature.]

Yes it would. That said, though, there is some advantage to using a cold one.

[Audience Member: They're attracted to the cold?]

Yes. That is an advantage. You're going to have to make the call on that.

[Audience Member: Depends on the individual? Or the person that you're treating?]

That's right. It has to—you don't want the experience to be a negative one for them, because they need to relax. So if you have a cold one you might even explain to them, "This is really good—this is a cold one." Take it out of their fridge, if they have it. If you're at their house, or something—it's a lot to get them to "buy in." You have to get them to "buy in." It's very important.

[Audience Member: And then you wrap it in the red and black yarn.]

Just wrap it around it. I don't completely cover it because it falls off—you know, just create a band or a binding. Like a belt around it. I've seen it done where they actually have the black and the red intertwined, where it's black, where it's red and black, or there's black and red intertwined.

Remember not to put this one in with your other eggs! [laughter] That's probably why they just wrapped it up anyhow! "Let's not make an omelette out of this one!" [laughter] Well, good luck with that.

You can also throw them in a river.

[Audience Member: I wanted to ask about putting the energy in the jar: are you talking about wiping your hand on the jar if you feel there's a lot of energy? Or are you talking about something that you think is in the room?]

Something in the room.

[Audience Member: Well, how do you get something in the room to go into the jar?]

If it's that condensed where you can feel it in this part of the room but not this one, you can—

[Audience Member: I think she's saying: "what's the

bait?"]

[Audience Member: Where's the bait?]

[Audience Member: Where's the bait? Is it actually in the jar?]

[Audience Member: Can you put M&Ms in the bottom of the jar?]

[Audience Member: A classic Taoist technique uses the jar-trapping thing. They'll use a talisman. They'll write out a talismant—just like any talisman, remember, is holding the vibration of that thing. So like attracts the like. They take that talisman and they put it in the jar.]

Yes.

[Audience Member: And so whatever the energy is that's attracted to that talisman just like instead of calling it down from wherever and putting it into your talisman here—you just leave it there and be as neutral as possible. It's attracted to that talisman. Once you feel the shift has changed, you're just capping it off. Sealing it again.]

[Audience Member: Because you're going to gravitate to the energy—]

[Audience Member: They're going to go to the thing that's the most comfortable body for them.]

Yes, and they throw salt in the jar though, too, and cap it. Or have salt. Some people have salt ahead of time. Which of course is kind of pushing it, because they don't *like* the salt, so that's kind of pushing it out, and if they end up catching it—it's kind of like me chasing you with a net. You're going to run away from me because I have a net. But if I end up catching you, you're not going to like it. So they'll put salt in the jar and this is a threat, basically. "If you continue to stay here and bother us, this is where you're going to end up." You're going to be in the "time-out" room. This is their version of the brass box.

[Audience Member: You remember—now, the younger ones aren't going to remember this, but—*Chitty Chitty Bang Bang*? Remember the child-catcher?]

That's it. That's what you're doing here.

[Audience Member: That's it—it's: "Free fireworks! All free today!"Then you get into the place with all the sweets, and then—]

[Audience Member: You're caught.]

[Audience Member: If Swiss chocolate's in there—]

Hey, if you've got something that likes Swiss chocolate, it's probably your friend. [laughter]

[Audience Member: So, would you need to know what's in there in order to make the proper talisman? Or do you use a generic—]

[Audience Member: You can, but you can get a generic one. You can figure out a generic one. Because you're not always going to know exactly what it is. This is the difference between your work and client work. You go to a client that says: "Oh, crap, you know, I did this thing, I did this ritual, I found this book" blah, blah, blah, "I invoked this thing" or evoked this thing, and now my life is shit and everything is going da, da, da. You get in there and you feel what it is—first I always ask them what it is. What did they do? And if it's that, then I'm making a talisman for that at the right time, and using that as a channel or a portal back to where its home is. Remember our normal everyday "license to depart"? "Peace between you and us." Go back to where you live. It's a portal—it's a place to send them back. It's not my job to torture the hell out of them. My job is to get it and then remove it to a place where it can be out of every person's life and surroundings. It's an act of compassion, it's not an act of war.]

That's really important because generally you begin with this school, this notion I taught you to put salt in the jar and kind of go after the thing. It's like chasing it with a net. It's probably going to run away, and if you catch it then it was too slow. Or you've got a problem, and—you had a problem to begin with, now you've just got a different type of problem. This is not "old school." You're not "slugging it out."

You're not slugging it out. That's not the purpose here. Something that we didn't do but—do you have those bottles?

[Audience Member: Yes.]

Great—we're going to hand them out. We have some glass bottles here—I like them, they're nice—Mike was very generous to help empty them. [raucous laughter]

We're going to hand these out—that way it's our version of recycling. This is a strange little piece known as a "witch bottle."

They find them stuck up chimneys in Appalachia, you know; they're pretty common. They've found a few recently in old houses in England.

[Audience Member: In Tennessee they bury them in the ground of an enemy.]

Yes. What they do is they fill them with all sorts of shiny and sharp and nasty things. The notion is that this energy, because it is Air-like, as it begins to condense, and vaporize, and be more congealed, it also has limits.

As it becomes more material, it can no longer simply pass through material things as it once could. So then it seeks an opening, and where's the greatest opening in your house? It would have been your chimney at one point. So vaporous ghosts enter through your chimney because you've salted your windowsill, and they won't go through there. Then they would put them there to keep them away. They're filled with all sorts of broken glass, rocks, nails—

[Audience Member: Iron nails.]

If you have any nails then drop one of each in for me. The old iron ones are my favorite, but anything will do. And why? We say spirits don't like iron. You see that in the Orient, too, the unearthly things don't like iron because it *cuts* and it I. Think of it this way: if you have smoke, and a lot of it, and it's just going all over the place, and you've got two big fans in your hand (like Oriental fans), you're going to try and congeal this smoke—you think I mean metaphorically here, but I mean *literally*. What's the last thing you would want?

Someone else coming in and waving something else around, right? Because there comes a point when the energy densifies. There comes a point when the tangibility takes place.

We talked about this "light" or this "energy"—I read you that quote that said that the "spiritus mundi," this etheric energy out there, this energy that fills the world, that fills all creation, can be made tangible and visible even though it is invisible. You've all seen it. Think of the auras that you've seen—the psychic phenomena. Some of the work you've done with Brian—I don't know a lot of it, I only know what's related to what he and I go over—but I know I was in lodge rooms years ago where that would be one of the demonstrations that would be done. It is "we're turning on the lights" to show that this is *real*. Part of that demonstration, too, was for those involved in it years ago, as it had not been done in that lodge for nearly seventy years.

I was asked to do a particular class in which we had to work with the actual manipulation of this energy in a tangible way. The first thing that begins to form is *lights*. These lights move in a kind of spiral pattern. Next you begin to see a slight fog. The color varies; it's usually kind of like a grey or bluish-grey, and it's thin like cigarette smoke. At that point it usually disperses. Then, using a great deal of effort—not too much, but just enough—you have to begin to extract it from the surrounding environment, condense it, and make it spin, so that it becomes dense.

Most people don't get that far. What they may get is a very distinct "sense" of a location—in front of them, or in the room—meaning that: there may not be the visible phenomena, but there are somatic phenomena.

Remember, we all process this differently. So even working with the somatic phenomena—which is probably more deeply rooted to the unconscious—you could still continue. When that energy is made dense enough, there are specific directions you go in and specific things you do. We will not be going over that today.[2]

You actually have now a tangible location in the room in which you know something is there. Now, if someone's really good they can actually bring it to a condition like that of a hologram. Most of the time what you've just done is you've created a nice kind of portal for different kinds of psychic projections, attunement, that kind of thing. But it is a very dense phenomena, and if not captured—if you have a means of capturing it—you can hold on to that for a while. If not, it will disperse naturally. That dispersal process is very common. So these beings—especially these, we'll say, "demonic" ones—are always in a constant state of dispersal; they're very chaotic. They're trying to create a center, but they don't *want* a center. They're very conflicted. That's why you get rid of them in this way.

The extraction of the energy in this practice—this experiment, if you will—is from the immediate environment. That's why, when you feel "cold spots," it's because the energy is extracted from the immediate environment. Sometimes you'll feel cold spots for reasons that aren't immediately obvious. I remember, years ago, I was doing a healing on a friend of mine. He had asked for it; I said, "Yeah, sure, why not?" And the temperature must have dropped about fifteen degrees. I can't tell you why. I have no idea why. I said: "Well, that's not good. Let's stop—we'll come back to this." So when you get those cold spots, if they're a physical place in a building that doesn't go away, then you've got a slightly different problem.

But if you are feeling them occasionally, particularly around people, or they are feeling them on occasion around rooms—somebody goes into this room and it feels cold—or "it's just that place, right there," localized—that's what we're talking about. That's because something is pulling energy from the environment.

---

[2]For more information on this topic, see Mark Stavish, *Mind of Hermes: Visionary Experiences in Western Esotericism* (IHS Study Guide Vol. VI, 2017).

[Audience Member: What did you do about it?]

Well, we just stopped and it went away. It never re-occurred, so it wasn't a problem. Now, on the other hand, I had a friend at about the same time who was involved in a variety of magical practices because he wanted to have some familiars to help him out. He was visiting, once. I said to my very young (and charming and often all-too-stupid!) friend, 'You know, it's really not too good of an idea. Why don't you get rid of them? Just get rid of them.'

That night they paid me a visit. I get up out of my bed and I walk out into my living room and—there they are. These three entities. The appearance is not so much one as if I'm looking at you. They appear as if I am looking in your direction, and a very ever-so-faint, "hologram" of you is there. I can see through you, but you're still there, or some shadowy essence is. There were three of them, and I said, "Oh, this is very interesting." I then told them: "Now it's time to leave." They didn't like that. I explained to them that it was time to leave NOW, and they did *not* like it. When they don't like it, what they try to do is to scare you—and saying "trying to scare you" is polite. [laughter]

[Audience Member: What did you do?]

You don't have to do anything, because they're raw emotion. We'll want to talk about that in a second. I said, "Okay, we'll play that game." And I remembered some mantras—for lack of a better term—some words that my great-uncle had taught me years earlier, and promptly they disappeared. They went very quickly. I then told my friend the next morning; I said, "I suggested that you get rid of these guys." I described to him what they were like, the various sizes and unique personality characteristics. Remember, it is an emanation, a vibration, and so you pick up the information very quickly. It's not like you have to do an interview. In your daily life there's some people who just present [snapping fingers] who they are. They're not hiding anything. That can be wonderful too, you know, in the beginning—it's the same thing with these things, often. He was a little surprised—he apologized. I said, "Well don't apologize; just get rid of them and don't do it again." He was surprised that I could actually describe their size and shape, their hierarchical relationship to each other and their characteristics. They have a relationship.

[Audience Member: These are entities that he brought in?]

Yes. So when you encounter them it's going to be all of a sudden; it's not going to be within the benefits of the confines of a magical circle. Of course, I'd just gotten out of bed for this. So it's not when you're in your best place.

I talked a lot yesterday about compassion and the role of compassion and helping people, though, unfortunately, when we do that it's really best to do it anonymously for a variety of reasons. One of those reasons is that *things often push back*. How often in life have you tried to help someone only to find that they really didn't want it? They say they do; but then you do it and what happens? "Oh, no, I gotta change. I don't wanna change! I want everything to go just right, but I don't wanna change!" [laughter] "Well, can't we just do this instead? Because it's easier!" [laughter] Enough. We can change. And when you generate a lot of compassion for people—you've probably seen this; you've probably heard it. "Oh, he's just so nice!" Or: "She's just so nice! Oh, I just hate them." [laughter]

When you start reading the Solomonic texts (and I'll bet before that, but that's probably when they first started writing it down), you'll see many talismans geared toward keeping the practitioner from the end result of envy, or bad influence back.

It's simply to remind you that that's why we wish the best for everyone. By the way, before this, I remember John saying once that he knew the seminar had to be important because there were just so many obstacles they encountered trying to get here. [laughter] Over the last two weeks it's just been amazing, what I've had to deal with. A few nights ago

I was getting out of my car and I ran into someone that I knew. I would generally make pleasantries and then continue about my business. For some reason, I said, "Oh, how are things going?" Which, you know, even before it was out of my mouth, I'm saying, "Why am I asking this? This is going to take me an hour!" An hour? And I mean an hour! You know the type?

And it doesn't matter what the weather is.

They'll stand there in the rain. Okay—there's got to be a reason for this. Let's see if I can figure it out. When I say a "reason"—we often don't pay enough attention to this—we over-intellectualize it. So he began to tell me what was going on, and quickly, very quickly, we spiraled into—without going into details—the "relationship ills" that he was involved with. As he did this I could see through his physical posture and through his breathing, his words, everything, that he was re-enacting this whole thing right in front of me. In fact, a part of me began to wonder if he actually knew that I was standing there and didn't think that I was the very person he was angry at, because he was so involved in the process. When he went into detail about the argument, I said, "Okay," and then, "I see."

We have a bunch of people who are five, six, seven years old. They're stuck. They're stuck in this kind of infantile argument. That's too bad. Well, let's see—maybe we can defuse this a little bit. So he made some statements that were very legitimate, and I said, "Well, yeah, that's a legitimate concern. You know, I mean, I can see how you can be upset about that." Nothing's happened. Howitzer—it's like a machine gun [machine gun firing sounds mimicked]. But the agreement broke in for a second, he paused, then he started up again. See the "pause" is your only window of opportunity. [laughter] That's why you have to create as many of them as possible and then try to interject your message. That's just a hypnotic rhythm thing, but it's the same in everyday communication.

[Audience Member: Did he ever ask you how you were doing?]

No—are you kidding me? [laughter]

[Audience Member: Just wanted to see how bad it was.]

[Audience Member: At least you got in "hello"!] [raucous laughter]

So—you're all familiar with it.

He continued with his "re-enactment." And I said, "You know what? I really have to try and help him here because if he goes home like this, this is going to be really bad for a lot of people." So I figured this has got to be probably why I just asked him—to see if we could defuse this a little. I don't know why—I can't tell you why—but the color of "pink" came to mind. Let's just send this guy some compassion here—some altruistic, defusing, pink energy. I sent him baby pink, baby-girl pink. And, for a second, his breathing slowed down, he stopped, and he stepped back. And then he stepped forward again, even louder. Even more intense.

So I mirror his body language a little bit—to develop a little more rapport—listen to him make a grievance, he agrees, legitimate statement. You'll always say something that's partially agreeable or completely, only out of proportion. You use that as your leverage in. So I make agreement; I say, okay—baby blue. I don't know why, it just came up. Not going to analyze it. Same thing. He pauses, breathes again, he steps back, he comes back again, but it's a little lower. So we go back and forth like this for a while—and he doesn't know what's going on. I'm not even there. He's just in his "rant" mode. You get it—you know what I'm talking about. I'm not even there. I just keep going with this until he gets at least to a point where I think or hope that he can at least go home and there won't be an explosion.

We can't fix it—but at least we can defuse it.

Very often this is all we do. You have to be okay with that. It's like when we send out these wonderful thoughts of world peace—we see what happens. The world is still a violent, crappy place. All we're doing is defusing what probably would have been a lot worse—and you have to be okay with that. You're just putting out fires. That's all. And it's okay. Because, if he did go home, chances are good it would have been pretty ugly. You just have to be okay with that.

Sometimes, again, it's not what *I* want for them, it's what they're capable of achieving and what I'm capable of giving. Each to their own capacity. Remember that from yesterday? Each to their own ability. Too often we either overestimate what people are capable of or we underestimate it. We have to step back and try and decide what is really possible. What are the real outcomes that we can get?

[Audience Member: Let me just ask something about that. So, one of the practices that I learned with that was that any time something happens to me—anything where I think that I'm on the brown end of the stick, right?—is that it's just a conditioned thing. It's not something that's inherent in me, or that I had all along; it's a conditioning constantly, constantly, constantly, any time I could think of it, I would put it back in and do this again. It's not the other person, you know? It's my inability to access where they are and what their abilities are, their "pluses" or "minuses." It has nothing to do with "they're doing this to me" or "they're doing that to me." I just failed to evaluate accurately what they were capable of.]

An honest self-assessment.

You know we dramatize this. We wage spiritual, magical, shamanic "wars against evil," but we're really just a bunch of dramatists. [chattering sound of wild animal heard]

[Audience Member: Possum?]

Something in the wall?

[Audience Member: Raccoon.]

[Audience Member: Raccoons, probably.]

Do we need to get rid of it?

[Audience Member: Nothing we can do.]

There's always something we can do. [laughter] Just matters whether it's going to smell in a few days! [laughter]

[Audience Member: Yeah, it's something—]

[animal-chattering heard, louder]

I kind of like this! [laughter] You know, this really fits the chamber well! [laughter] It's okay.

With the drama, there's a tendency to use a lot of language that doesn't really accurately describe what's going on. We like labels because of the way they sound. We have to at some point free ourselves of those labels. That doesn't mean we ditch them completely with others; it's part of tradition when you're teaching, you teach certain things. But then at some point you say, "You know what? This is simply about my failure to adequately assess the situation." That's all it is. Whether it was a plumbing error or whether it was a business error or whether it was what was going on in the relationship. It's just—okay. What did I come into it with? And what did I leave it with? That's it. So we have to make sure that we can—I don't like the idea of what we're calling it—but you just take responsibility for what's going on. Because clearly the other person—they can't. If they could, then they wouldn't be in that relationship with you of asking you to fix "XYZ."

So, amongst ourselves, we have to be very clear with our language in the discussion. We save the flowery rhetoric for prayers and invocations.

Now, they have something that are called "witch balls." Witch balls are of two kinds: I've seen them where they're wonderful glass balls that are filled in the same way, or sometimes they're glass balls that are reflective. There seem to be two different definitions of this. One is very similar to what we have here, and along with that I've heard the idea of those that are just for the "dog and pony" show. We hang them in the room because they look nice and people think, "Oh, they're spirit balls!" Whether that's true or not.

One of the other definitions is of a malignant entity, specifically a malignant thought form sent by someone else, specifically and intentionally. These balls, if you see them, are just that: they're like these nasty sphere of everything negative. Sharp and coarse and brittle—all things *not* nice, because that's not what the person was thinking of when they were thinking of you (or whomever).

I'm sure they can manifest spontaneously in your environment, a collective people doing it unconsciously. I have no doubt about that. I encountered one many years ago on a very long road-trip—three thousand miles round-trip where I had to make a delivery down to Miami. It was quite fascinating when it finally revealed itself, because the psychological state that you're in is that time and space are very much distorted. This was not just the effect of driving. This had happened before I had undertaken the trip. I was actually glad to go on the trip because I knew something was really pretty wrong. Something was very wrong. And I probably didn't eat for about ten days. And it didn't bother me at all. I had very little sleep for about that same period, and it didn't bother me at all. But the neurotic, undifferentiated anxiety was the dominant theme. One night it was in the hotel that I stayed in halfway back; I saw this thing, "in and out." The question is, where is it coming from? Why? I never figured that out; I never found out. I was able to defuse it and then moved on.

It's a fairly unpleasant experience, you know. I'm not telling you this because it's like "war stories"—it's a very unpleasant experience, and many of you have been experiencing that kind of undifferentiated anxiety lately. A lot of other people have as well—they find out they are just anxious. When this kind of coalesces, it is shape and form.

[Audience Member: Can I ask you a question? When you're "in it," sometimes it's hard to get into your toolbox if you're not sure of the best way to defuse it, because you have to first identify whether it's from you or it's coming from outside. So do you have any special technique for defusing, when you're in that state? One or the other?]

No, you just have to cut the anxiety down before it arises, because it comes and goes in waves. It's like normal life, only intensified. See, it's not a "special" experience—it's a daily experience that you have, but the anxiety goes like that [snapping fingers]. Now, the anxiety's amplified, expanded. You have to cut it down before it arises, before it envelops you—and it's not easy. That's the point—it's not easy; if it were easy, we wouldn't be here.

But we practice it, and the way you do it is in daily life—you don't let your neurotic tendencies overrun you. You don't gossip; you don't criticize. Don't be nit-picky. Complaining. You have to have a positive attitude about things, and *find* the positive. Focus positively on yourself, not negatively, and focus positively on others. I mean here that you should encourage their strengths rather than pointing out their weaknesses. Constructive critique. Constructive—so before we say anything we ask ourselves, "What good does this do?" Who does this benefit? When I have to do an analysis of many unpleasant things to find out why things are going on, I have to ask that, too: who benefits from this? Someone's getting a payoff somewhere. What is that payoff? Who is it? How do they get it?

But for us, we're not dealing with that. We're dealing with just being kinder and being gentler and being nicer to one another. Being gentler—more refined. Being gentlemen and gentlewomen. You don't want to be coarse and awful all the time. It can be fun—you know that. [chuckling] There's advantages, right? But not all the time. Paracelsus was wonderful, but that was one of his downfalls: he was simply never able to overcome that in his dealings with people.

[Audience Member: Maybe that's because we don't get a lot of sleep doing this work.]

Maybe. [laughter] Could be—and of course you want to kind of smooth out the edges: symbolism of the masonic ashlar. The rough stone made smooth—the rough ashlar to the smooth ashlar.

[Audience Member: So with all the anxiety of the "coming of the end," there's chaos going on around us. Not necessarily with us—I don't feel it's within what I'm experiencing, but I see a lot of it. It's: "Oh my god! It's coming up! And my calendar's over!" How do we help defuse that?]

What are you afraid of? You just ask them directly: what are you afraid of? "The world's gonna end!" No it won't. The world will still be here. It won't explode. Even if the corona—as someone says—raised the temperature to two hundred and twenty degrees, and all human life disappears, the world will still be here. Oh, but *you* won't! So what are you afraid of? [whispered] "You're gonna die." Well, yeah!

[Audience Member: You're going to die anyway—]

Well that's the point of the thing—well, yeah! I mean, when did you expect that *not* to happen? When did you expect that not to happen? We're all a little disappointed about it, but—different people, they're often so good at just avoiding the question, you've got to nail them down with it. When did you expect not to die? Okay. Now we get to the real question. The opposite side is: what's the payoff? You have other people who are preparing for all sorts of things—and I'm a firm believer in being prepared, being a Boy Scout. There's no reason any of you should not have ample supplies of food and water and water filtration, available medical supplies to you—because if this were a hundred years ago, that would have been normal. If it were seventy years ago in many places of the country, it would have been normal. Only now because we have—just in time—things drop out of the sky, it's magical, the seven-thousand-mile supply chain from China. We think that that's normal. It's normal to get up on a Sunday morning and go down to the grocery store and get what we want to eat. I recall the "Blue Laws." We would have to wait until afternoon or midday, I think it was, in order to get on our bikes and ride over to the drug store—it's limited, too. Drug stores, gas stations—most of them were privately owned, so they weren't open. And I think grocery stores were the only things allowed to be open after church.

And we've come to expect this notion of "whatever I want whenever I want it," and that's okay, as long as you realize that's not a permanent state. [chuckling] And that can change. Now, many of you have had friends or relatives whose lives have been affected by the recent storm. It hit the east coast, in Jersey, in New York, and that area. Many people did not prepare, many people—even though they had weeks of warning—many people didn't believe it would be that bad, many people thought, "I live in a flood plain, but might not have to put anything above three feet." Or, "Why do it at all?" Many people didn't do anything except wait to become a victim—and then complain. Now we don't want to admit to that, because that's not a good story.

[Audience Member: It doesn't get any money from FEMA.]

It doesn't get you FEMA money. But if you think the federal government's going to come to your aid, you're out of your mind, because it's not really their job—it's like the police department. The police department's job is not to protect you. It's to protect the *community*. *You* are not the community—the Supreme Court said that. You can't sue the police department for not showing up to your house when it's getting burglarized in the middle of a riot. Their job is the "common good." So, this is part of growing up; it's taking responsibility for yourself. As you do that, you're able to help others. You've got something to help them with—not just something internally, but something tangibly as well. No reason for you not to have three months of food in your house. I've worked in stores; I've worked in things—supply chains that drop [snapping fingers], and they're there like that. If you have the disruption of a week or two, though (which I've seen) you're okay—but your neighbors aren't.

So, that's what people are afraid of. They know that their life hangs on a thread, on all levels, and they're terrified of it, because they haven't thought about anything else. They have not given any conscious thought to their mortality or to their immortality. It's all just sensory stuff. Not that there's anything wrong with "sensory stuff"—we're part of it—but it's JUST that, and you don't know what else to do if you're in a trap. So you've got a lot of people who are "prepping" because they know that the world is basically "decadent," and they're waiting for it to end so that they can establish their version of "heaven on earth" and whatever their "utopia" is going to be.

We have others who just simply hate their jobs or their lives or whatever it is, and they're too cowardly to do something different.

So that when the boundaries break down around them, because they can't break through them, they can go kill zombies or something like that—or whatever they think they're going to do. I don't know what these things are that they're going to do. They'll be—the "new Messiah."

But all this is neurotic—all this is pathological. It all comes down to simply not wanting to be responsible for myself, or responsible to others. That's all it comes down to. Not accepting that, well, you know, life is short. How short? Well, do the math. As I said to many of you: come on, let's do the math here. Stop screwing around. What are you worried about? "Yeah, we've got bills to pay." We all have bills to pay. See that's part of the selfishness—I've got one friend, very wonderful fellow, whom I like a great deal, but terribly selfish. Lots of fun, but—why do you need to act like you're special? I have far more responsibilities than you do—why do you complain so much? And he's like—no, seriously, I'm just asking you a serious question, I mean honestly, I mean for years now—you're talented, you got all this going for you, you've got a great salary. Goddamn, boy! You're a whiny little wimp! [laughter] You got anything down there? Or are you a Ken doll?

So, like this guy, I've got to be a little nicer to him, because he's so angry—this guy's so unmotivated. You don't get an emotional response out of him. Deep inside, though, there's a lot of anger. He's really angry. So among other things he's really angry, too. So if I can stir that a little bit, I might be able to help him identify what the real source of his anger is. It's a project. And I don't want to make him a project. Don't make people your projects. [laughter]

My point is very simple. He's a great guy, really smart, a lot going for him, but the anger, keeps him down. The other guy's explosive in his anger. Literally, physically explosive. This one internalizes it. Just pushes it all down, which creates a condition where he's inert. He neuters himself—literally. He's unable to act. So with that comes a whole bunch of other things I don't want to go into, because that's a whole different class, but—it's like, when you look at the people around you—I bring these up so you will look at the people around you—what's the payoff? What's the payoff?

[Audience Member: And these guys know what you do for work, right?]

Yes. One more than others. And the payoff is, well, again, when you're looking at people with this "2012" thing, and this neurotic behavior, it all comes down to: "I'm afraid to take responsibility for my life." I'm afraid to act like a big boy. I'm afraid to act like a big girl. That fear—that need for safety— that need for external confirmation is crippling. Crippling. All of these things may happen—the world is simply changing places, unstable; we don't know what will happen from one place, time to time, to the next. These prophecies may or may not come true, but it doesn't change the fact that I have to be responsible for my life, and make plans. What they want is a *guarantee*. "Please tell me what will happen so I can plan accordingly." I can't tell you what will happen so you can plan accordingly.

Well, actually, I *can* tell you what will happen so that you can plan accordingly: you're going to die. Doesn't matter how much you own or how much you owe, you're going to die. So, figure out what you're going to do between now and then, because it can come at any time. Here—that's what's going to happen. [chuckling]

[Audience Member: That way you only have to memorize one speech.]

Right. [laughter] And we can dress that up—we can dress that up and polish it as much as we want. But it's the same thing. Some people respond to that nicely; some people respond to it not-so-nicely. But that's really what we're getting at. Because behind the "2012" stuff is a whole bunch of ideas about "spiritual welfare." Yes, he's going to save us: Sky God or Sky Daddy or Earth Mommy. And then we're going to all get along and sing "Kumbaya." [chuckling] It's so perfectly infantile—it's symbolic of the whole, neurotic thought process. Really.

[Audience Member: They're the end of the spectrum of the neurotic.]

Yes. It won't happen. And because these states are states of mind—there are prophecies and predictions that are very unpleasant, and may continue to unfold that way. However, that's not the point. Whether it's the Second Coming of Jesus, whether it's the First or whatever Multiple Comings of the Messiah, whether it's the Thirteenth Imam, or whatever—the Maitreya Buddha, the four hundred years at the end of the Kali Yuga—the story's all the same. And the point of the story, at the end of time, so to speak, is that each and every one of us has to be responsible, right now, for what we do.

What we do *right now*. That's it. And if you can open yourself up courageously to the reality of the unstable environment in which you live, and the fact that it *is* unsafe, and it is unstable, and that you're the only one who can take care of yourself or ensure your salvation, then you're well on your way to adulthood. To step into wonderfully, politically incorrect land here just for the sake of a grand illustration—and you know when we illustrate points we always go to extremes, too—that's the point why, because it's so dramatic, it's black on white, or white on black, whatever—but as many of you know I occasionally teach on the university level and trying to

explain to young men and young women that people perceive
you based upon how you dress, is *very difficult*. They say,
"Well, I should be able to do whatever I want." And I say, "Yes
you can—you can do whatever you want. You can do exactly
whatever you want. Anything. That's okay. You just have to
take responsibility for it. And realize that if you're coming in
for a job—an interview—and you've got more tattoos than
clothes, that that limits your possibility for employment. You
just have to be okay with that."

They say, "Well, what do you mean?" I say, "You've got
all the lectures on multiculturalism, right?" "Oh, yeah." "Well,
guess what? There was a time when the only people who
had tattoos were gangsters, whores, and mercenaries. And
slaves. So, I have to ask myself, if I hire you, am I going to
put you with one of my Japanese clients where the guys that
they see with tattoos are either prostitutes or gangsters?"
I'm just being inclusive here—I'm not being judgmental. I
just have to wonder how, since they're paying the bills, how
they're going to react. And then they say, "Oh, okay." And
then it goes down to other things. See, how you present
yourself, again, is an unconscious image of what you value,
presented to the world. On the other hand, when you go to
a business meeting, you dress in a particular way because
you are making a conscious decision of how you will present
yourself to the board. When you dress up for ritual you're
making a conscious effort concerning how you present yourself
to the invisible world, to the universe. Do you understand?

I'm okay with what you do. So the one guy says: "That's
great, but, you want to walk down that street at two in
the morning—dressed like that?" I said: "That's fine. Just
understand—[thumping sound]—you *will* be solicited." He
goes: "What?" I said: "Men will ask to pay you for sex."
[laughter] I said: "You also run the risk in this neighborhood
of becoming a victim. So, you can do that if you want—but
I want you to understand: that's not the place to do it. Nor
at that time." "But I should be able to do whatever I want!"

"You *can* do whatever you want; just understand: other people are going to be reacting to that. And they're going to see you differently. And they will see you according to how you present yourself, at times and places." It's very complex. This is far more complex than you realize. I said: "If you were in a club, that would be great. I know it's only two blocks over—trust me. [laughter] There is a line—you've just crossed from one world into the next and you don't even know it. You don't live here—you're just a visitor."

And that's the way it is in our psychic environments, too: we don't live there, we're just visitors! And we're crossing from one world into the next.

[Audience Member: That's a really good analogy, actually.]

We've got to make sure that we're dressed appropriately.

[Audience Member: So we complain.]

Yes. And that dress is—

[Audience Member: It's our life.]

Yes. Our thought, our word, our deed.

[Audience Member: You've got to think positive.]

These are generalities. I can give exceptions to this rule, too. But these are just a broad generality, just to kind of "bring out," to illustrate, graphically, the point I'm trying to make.

✠   ✠   ✠

◇ APPENDIX ◇

Offering Prayers

ORPHIC HYMN

Hearken divinities, you who hold the reins of sacred wisdom—who set men's souls on fire with flames indomitable, drawing them through the cloudy depths far up to the immortals,

Purging us with mystic rites of indescribable hymns;

Hearken great saviors! From divine books, grant me the innocent, blameless light that dissipates the clouds so I may discover the truth about man and his immortal divinity!

Neither let evil working spirits restrain me under the Lethean water of oblivion, ever far from the blessed, for my soul would no longer continue to stray,

Nor suffer the cruel pains of imprisonment in the bonds of life!

Nay, gods of high and illustrious wisdom, Masters and leaders hear me, the hastener along the Upward Way! Initiate me into the orgiac mysteries and reveal them by the ceremonies of sacred words!

OFFERING PRAYER

Sophia, all-encircling goddess, whose embrace with the All-Father gives rise to pure desire, and birth to all the worlds and their children. Your tender kiss renews all life and stirs our sleeping mind to awakening, moving us from ignorance and suffering to wisdom and bliss.

Accept this our fleshy offering, and bless it so that all the demons and guardians who dwell here joyfully receive it, and their happiness clears away all obstacles from our Path and that they defend us on our way.

Bless this sweet drink that the ghosts who wander through our domain are satisfied, their hunger and thirst quenched, turning their sorrow into joy, so that they may be guided and guide others upwards on their Path of Return.

Bless this our perfume, that those who wander in the heavenly realms, ascending and descending into the earthly realms, may hear our prayers and be justly guided into the Kingdom of Light, and hailed as returning Heroes, Conquerors of the Indomitable Citadel.

Bless this sacred wine, nectar of the gods, that the full power of life, Mercury, the eternally young and immortal one, Lord of the Two Lands, is eternally awakened within us, and that the demi-gods and angels pour forth their holy power into our Work and in turn be blessed with eternal life.

Bless this offering stone that it may bear witness to our sincerity and devotion to the Work, and that the powers of the Gods is born, raised, and lives eternally within me, it is in that which we live, move, and have our being. May all the archangels and gods know light eternal, and fear death no more.

Bless these offered jewels that all beings be blessed with health, wealth, capacity of mind, pure desire, and leisure to undertake the lightning path on their return to the Eternal.

Hear this our prayer, your children, your [sons/daughters].

Amen ✠ Amen ✠ Amen ✠

After completion, you may share the offerings with your altar deity, others present, and, lastly, consume them yourself. Some should be disposed of so that animals may enjoy them, and any bloody offerings (or anything red) should be set aside in a dark, distant, or wild place. It is traditional to have a small plate separate from the others (or a designated location on the main plate) upon which offerings for the demons and chaotic beings are placed. These latter offerings are then taken off and disposed of in a dark, distant, or wild place.

᪥ ✿ ᪥

Support from the Institute for Hermetic Studies

The Institute for Hermetic Studies is a non-profit organization offering a range of ongoing support to individual students and groups through online materials, seminars, and private tutorial. These include but are not limited to: basic, intermediate, and advanced instruction in the Hermetic Arts and Sciences, astrological consultations, assistance with psychic and spiritual crises, and training for ordination in the Minor and Major Orders of the Church of St. Cyprian the Mage of Antioch. All information regarding our programs is announced in our electronic newsletter VOXHERMES. For more information contact:

The Institute for Hermetic Studies
P.O. Box 4513
Wyoming, PA 18644-04513

www.hermeticinstitute.org
info@hermeticinstitute.org

Mark Stavish (Pennsylvania) is a respected authority in the study and practice of Western spiritual traditions. He is the author of numerous books, most recently *Egregores: The Occult Entities That Watch Over Human Destiny* (Inner Traditions, 2018), along with the IHS Monograph Series, IHS Ritual Series, and the preceding volumes of IHS Study Guides, as well as *The Magical World of Dr. Joseph Lisiewski, The Path of Alchemy, Kabbalah for Health and Wellness,* and *Between the Gates: Lucid Dreaming, Astral Projection, and the Body of Light in Western Esotericism.* His works have been translated into nine languages worldwide. He is founder of both the Institute for Hermetic Studies (Wyoming, Pennsylvania), where he is Director of Studies, and the Louis Claude de St.-Martin Fund, a non-profit fund dedicated to the study and practice of esotericism.

Alfred DeStefano III (Virginia) is Editor and Publication Manager of the various Institute for Hermetic Studies titles, overseeing all aspects of interior book design. In addition to his occupation as a college instructor of mathematics, he has assisted in the production of numerous esoteric works, including the most recent Seventh Edition of Israel Regardie's *The Golden Dawn,* edited by John Michael Greer (Llewellyn).

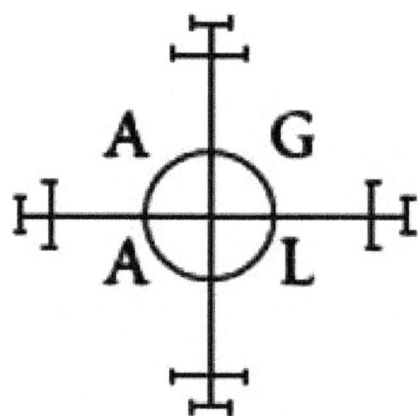

Printed in Dunstable, United Kingdom